Why Do I Do What I Don't Want to Do?

SPECIAL EDITION
FOR
WORLDWIDE PICTURES
1201 Hennepin Ave.
Minneapolis, MN 55403

Why Do I Do What I Don't Want to Do?

William Backus
&Marie Chapian

BETHANY HOUSE PUBLISHERS
MINNEAPOLIS, MINNESOTA 55438
A Division of Bethany Fellowship, Inc.

All Scripture quotations, unless otherwise noted, are taken
from the King James Version of the Bible.

Copyright © 1984
Marie Chapian and William Backus
All Rights Reserved

Published by Bethany House Publishers
A Division of Bethany Fellowship, Inc.
6820 Auto Club Road, Minneapolis, MN 55438

Printed in the United States of America

Library of Congress Cataloging in Publication Data

Backus, William D.
   Why do I do what I don't want to do.

   Sequel to: Telling yourself the truth.
    1. Christian life—1960—   2. Happiness.
I. Chapian, Marie.   II. Title.
BV4501.2.B253   1984   248.4'841   84–6336
ISBN 0–87123–625–7

The Authors

WILLIAM BACKUS, Ph.D., is a Christian psychologist and an ordained Lutheran clergyman. He is Founder and Director of the Center for Christian Psychological Services in Minneapolis, Minnesota. He and his family make their home in St. Paul, Minnesota, where he is also associate pastor of a large Lutheran church.

MARIE CHAPIAN, Ph.D., is the best-selling author of a long list of books including *Love and Be Loved, Telling Yourself the Truth* with William Backus, *Fun To Be Fit, Free To Be Thin* with Neva Coyle and *Staying Happy in an Unhappy World.* She is a psychotherapist, and before moving to California, served on the staff of Dr. Backus' clinic where she worked closely with him in developing Misbelief Therapy. Dr. Chapian travels widely as a popular seminar and conference speaker and is a well-known guest on Christian radio and television.

Table of Contents

Introduction

The Apostle Paul said, "For the good that I would I do not: but the evil which I would not, that I do" (Rom. 7:19). He posed the question that men and women have been asking for generations, "Why do I do what I don't want to do?"

After Dr. Backus and I collaborated on our first book together, *Telling Yourself the Truth*, we began work on this follow-up volume that would continue at the point where it left off. The counseling method we named "Misbelief Therapy" is changing the lives of thousands of people, and we are delighted with the overwhelming response from readers who write to us from all over the world. Translated into four languages, *Telling Yourself the Truth* is helping people make important changes in their attitudes towards themselves and others.

We are gratified at the number of professionals who employ Misbelief Therapy in their counseling practices. Many colleges and Bible schools around the world have made *Telling Yourself the Truth* re-

quired reading. Sunday school classes, home fellow-
ships, churches and Bible study groups are using it
with its accompanying Study Guide.

Mental and spiritual well-being cannot be complete without coming to grips with "Why Do I Do
What I Don't Want To Do?" Sin has been with us
since Adam and Eve, but that doesn't mean we have
to stand by helplessly as it ravages our lives. With
this book we want to help you identify the problem
and the source of defeating behaviors, the reason you
hurt yourself and remain trapped. With the powerful
principles revealed here, we believe you can be free
from the bondage of doing what you don't want to do.

Today can be a turning point in your life.

But just *knowing* principles is not enough. That
is why we've written this book as a work book, a
guide and counselor to help lead you to a time of
discovery and change.

You can reach your full potential and experience
peace and a loving sense of contentment as you learn
more about yourself and why you do what you don't
want to do. Our professional colleagues will notice a
lack of scientific terminology in this book; we specifically avoided psychological phraseology so that all
our readers will understand and feel at home with
what we are saying.

We ask our pastor friends, fellow therapists and
counselors to join us in the discovery of how to conquer the misbeliefs which bind many of God's children. It is our deepest longing to see each one who
has ever looked up to a loving heavenly Father to
live a wholesome, happy life, free from sin and guilt
and bondage.

Marie Chapian
William Backus

CHAPTER ONE

Whose Fault Is It?

In the Gilbert and Sullivan musical, "Princess Ida," there is a very disagreeable character named King Gama. He has no interest in life except to make trouble for other people. King Gama criticizes, insults, and hurts people for the sole purpose of making them feel terrible.

Another king in the story decides to punish him. After considering what the worst punishment could be for such a person, he decides upon the most cruel one of all—to give the man everything he wants. When King Gama has received all he wants, he becomes dreadfully bored and even more unhappy than he had been before. His predicament is worse than ever because now he has nothing to complain about.

11

Now that he has everything as he has always wanted it to be, he is miserable.

Now let's change our focus from King Gama to you. What do you blame *your* unhappiness on? To whom do you accredit your dissatisfaction? Maybe you answer, "It's my husband," or "It's my lack of a husband," or "It's my financial situation," or "It's my children." Maybe you blame your troubles on the suspicion that God isn't doing what He is supposed to be doing. God should be doing what *you* want Him to—shouldn't He?

You are right in suspecting there's a culprit who causes your distress, but the truth is, the culprit is probably yourself. You make yourself unhappy.

Have you ever wondered why you are always surprised when something bad happens? Have you ever been upset about things that are completely out of your control? Does news of tragedies, such as earthquakes, tornados, volcanic eruptions, or floods unnerve and distress you? Maybe you have the dream that things should be perfect, that justice should be flawless, but if you measure events and circumstances according to what is fair or unfair, you discover there is a lack of justice in the world. After living in a world such as this, you should begin to expect injustice and thus not go to pieces when you encounter it. But you don't.

The only perfect thing in life is truth—which only God can show to us. The human race tends to be made up of liars; we are surrounded by liars. Even we who are Christians will habitually twist and distort the truth. If something bad occurs, we think we are being persecuted or that we are suffering some sort of godly disablement for a holy purpose.

How can we pinpoint and deal with these dis-

crepancies we have in our view of life? The first way
is to analyze our view of the truth.

Beauty by Any Other Name . . .

If we look around us and see our world as unattractive, what tells us it is unattractive? In order to
make a value judgment between what is attractive
and what is not, or what is ugly and what is not, we
need to have a concept of beauty. But how do we
acquire a concept of beauty in the midst of imperfection? No human has ever seen perfect beauty. We
have seen many beautiful things, but the closer we
look at a beautiful thing the more defects we find. So
what do we use as our model for beauty?

This is the point at which Christian thought sep-
arates from non-Christian thought. The secular hu-
manists diagnose the trouble with people as "society." This philosophy says that people get warped
personalities, get into trouble, become neurotic, because of society's structure. They claim that the injustices in society produce chaos in people's lives.
Secular journalists even write editorials claiming our
problem is Bible-based Christianity which has per-
meated the society. Other critics falsely believe that
Christianity fosters bigotry and bigotry is our society's downfall.

The Word of God tells us what is wrong with society: *sin*. The problem is not conflict between human
instincts and structured society, not religious bigotry, but sin. Many churches don't even recognize
this truth.

Freud, Inner Healing and a Hole in the Head

Sigmund Freud believed man had a basic problem, but he ignored sin in his hypothesis. He taught that man's instincts do not measure up with what society expects of him, so therefore these two forces are always in collision. Inner conflict, Freud believed, is internalized by the person as a result of the training and conditioning received in childhood. Freud recognized a basic problem inherent in man, but he did not see the answer being man's separation from God.

Albert Ellis, another prominent psychologist, in one of his most memorable statements, said that he has never met a human being who did not have a large-sized hole in his head. Both Freud and Ellis tried to say that something is wrong with us. This "something wrong" is not just a trait of those people who are mental patients in hospitals or people who are having obvious, severe problems. Freud might say we have something wrong with us because all other people have a death wish, or he might say our instincts cannot attain to what society requires of us. Ellis explains that the large hole in our head needs to be filled with "positive growth stimuli" or it will program itself for destruction.

Our problem, however, is not society; not conflict between our instincts and the society; not a hole in the head; not only because of our childhood in which we were unloved or abused. Our problem is sin. Here is what we tell ourselves when we avoid the problem of sin:

1. Whatever is wrong with me it isn't my fault. (It's my childhood. It's society. It's life. It's hard knocks.)

2. Whatever is wrong with me is worthy of my deepest concern and despair. (I'm a poor victim of fate and my problems are the worst in the world. Nobody suffers as I do. If they do, I really don't care.)

3. The answer to my problems lies outside of my own abilities. (Someone else is responsible to make me feel better—and they had better hurry up and do it!)

You may tell yourself that someone else's love, tenderness and support will be the answer to your problems. That may be nice, but it is not the answer. It is not true that your well-being depends upon other persons or things (your environment) delivering good things to you. With such an outlook, you will never help yourself as you need to be helped. If all you need to do is run out and find somebody or something to make you happy, we counselors would have an easy time of it. But you've already tried it, and it doesn't work, does it? As with most people, you again and again look for answers outside yourself because you see your problems as due to life not treating you right. You think your problems are environmental.

Who controls your environment? God does—doesn't He? If God runs the environment and the environment is not treating you right, then God isn't doing a very good job of being God, is He? God, however, does not dictate every aspect of your environment. Certainly He created this world and oversees all that transpires, but He made man and nature to operate without His constant manipulation. He built physical laws into the universe and gives each person a free will. Unfortunately, man and nature are tainted and warped because of thousands of years of sin. The environment was designed perfectly and God would prefer it ran that way. But in order that He can have a love-relationship with those who desire it, He allows the human race to live as it pleases—within the wise limits He set up for our protection.

God doesn't waste time finding blame for problems. He gives people strategies for living happily. It is crucial to stop pinning the blame for your unhappiness on someone or something else. *You* are the one who is in control and *you* can change things. If you have convinced yourself that you do not need to overcome your sins, that God will do it for you, you are deceiving yourself.

Though there are many things in the Christian life that God does for you, there are many things that He will not do. One thing God will not do for you is *believe*. He creates your *ability* to believe but He won't do it for you. He will help you overcome sin, but He will not do it *for* you. Neither does God take up the sword of the Spirit for you. We do. The Bible says, *You* "put on the whole armor of God," and *You* "take . . . the sword of the Spirit" (Eph. 6:13, 17, NIV). Those words are an imperative, a command, on which to act.

Breaking the Sin Cycle

Each act of sin results from a cycle of events and actions. The first is the *antecedent stimulus*. This is what we mistakenly think *causes* us to sin. We may say, "Circumstances were so bad that I just gave up," or "God just doesn't seem to answer my prayers—that's why I'm drinking again," or "If it hadn't been for that sweet-smelling bakery, I never would have eaten that chocolate cake," or "I know I gave up smoking, but when I'm around people who are smoking I can't help having a cigarette."

Although we usually blame our emotions and our behavior on such antecedents, they are not the *cause* (an antecedent is something that occurs first and generates a response).

The second stage is our *belief about the antecedent.* If we believe that lustful thoughts, for instance, are good for us, even though God says they aren't, we will behave according to that belief. The following statements demonstrate misbelief: "It's awful that my wife makes me mad, so I have the right to get angry, act unreasonably and make a spectacle of myself," or "It's awful that I can't spend money as freely as I want to," or "It's awful that I'm not loved the way I crave to be loved," or "It's awful that God doesn't answer my prayers when I want Him to." Notice the frequent use of the word "awful." We lie often to ourselves using that word.

The third stage is the *behavior we engage in as a result of our belief,* which is what we tell ourselves about the antecedent. What we believe causes our response. If we believe it would be good for us to shoplift, go to an X-rated movie, lie about someone to boost our ego, or whatever, we will do it. If we believe something is good for us, we will do it, take it, have it or eat it. If we believe the wrong thing, our resultant behavior is sin.

The cycle of sin is all too familiar to you. It probably seems easier to give up than to fight. But you want victory. This is your opportunity to debate, argue and challenge the lie that sin is good. You probably have been taught it is not nice to argue or to challenge, but this is a fight in which no holds are barred. And you must take the initiative.

"*Believe* in the Lord Jesus, and you shall be saved"

(Acts 16:31, NIV). He doesn't do the believing for you. God also will not repent for you. You must do the repenting—the first step of victory over sin. If you sin, you can change your behavior. You can take the sword of the Spirit, which is the Word of God, and use it to conquer your misbeliefs. You can begin to remove those untruths by telling yourself, "I refuse to allow myself to indulge in this sin."

You can win the battle. If you are serious about being a victorious Christian, you know that a victorious person is a happier person because he is able to control himself.

Understanding the sin cycle which we have enumerated here will help you to overcome the lies which undergird all sin. Lying is the servant of most abnormal drives and rarely an isolated, single act. Lying denies what *is*. Lying is a way of life. *But so is truth*. God's truth gives us the final victory. There are no lies or deception in Him. God's truth, a reflection of His perfect love and power, will energize and liberate you.

Pray with us:

Heavenly Father, I open my heart and my mind in expectation. I fully expect to be joyfully blessed in every area of my life as I learn to conquer sin (however great or small). You said the truth would set me free and I choose to believe you. In Jesus' name. Amen.

CHAPTER TWO

Welcome to Freedom

The eyes of the woman seated across the desk were filled with distress. She spoke to the therapist with a tearful voice. "I can't seem to find solutions to these problems of mine," she said. "It seems as though I'm caught in a trap with no way out." She took a deep breath and with a tone of heart-rending desperation pleaded, "Please tell me there is a way to turn the bad into good."

Many people feel there is no way out of the swamp of sin and its resulting pain and guilt. We find among many of our patients a feeling of powerlessness over their own behaviors. Many say, "I just don't know *why* I do such things," and, "Why can't I get control of my bad habits?"

Is Sin Really Fun?

Sin is not fun. It brings suffering, pain, destruction, poverty, alienation, and misery. Sin can even make people neurotic. Karl Menninger asks in his book, *Whatever Became of Sin?*, why psychologists always try to explain what's wrong with people in terms other than *sin*? Menninger explains sin is a fitting description for troubled human behavior. Senseless tragedies often occur because a person feels there is no escape from sin.

A deeply disturbed middle-aged man screamed from the ledge of the building before he jumped, "I can't stand my life! Hell will be a relief!" Onlookers watched in horror as he plunged six stories to the pavement below. Police revealed later through witnesses and photographs the sordid events which led to his demise. Wanted in over three states, the only solution he could think of was death. Bondage to sin had literally killed him.

This man died a senseless death. No one needs to continually live (and die) as a victim of sin. The power of God is available to you to overcome sin. The joy and happiness of victory is available to everyone, including you, and this book will show you how to gain it; it will not only show you how to overcome sinful habits in your life, but how to change your way of dealing with *temptation* to sin, as well.

Sin is always doing what your better senses don't really want to do. You think you need your pride or rage to protect yourself from pain, but your heart tells you you're safe in God. You're loved, protected and strengthened by His loving spirit. Why do you do what you don't want to do? Why do you hurt yourself by remaining in persistent bondage to defeating behaviors?

Let's begin with the realization that Jesus came into the world because we all need a cure for sin. Psychologist Dr. O. Hobart Mowrer created a furor among psychologists when he asserted that sin and guilt, not internal conflict and poor toilet training, were the root of human neuroses. And *Whatever Became of Sin?* was written by a psychiatrist, not a theologian.

God offers you the ability to overcome defeating behavior—not only its penalty but its *power* also. This book will give very practical methods for overcoming hurtful habits which may have been defeating you. In the past you have made many excuses for your defeat, but your situation is never beyond hope. God did not put you on this earth to spiritually hobble along in guilt and fear, telling yourself, "I'm just treading water," and "A loser like me can't expect much." Worst of all, you may be saying, "I just hope I can hang on until a brighter day comes, if that ever happens."

Why should you continue to live as a pawn of negative thinking when you have the power of God— the truth—which can enable you to overcome, to live a clean, happy and fulfilled life? You can do something about the problem of sin. Although you are not alone in your plight—"For all have sinned, and come short of the glory of God" (Rom. 3:23)—the terrific news for all of us is, "Sin shall not have dominion over you" (Rom. 6:14a). The power God has given to us to live in victory is the *truth*, which "shall set you free."

The Lie

Carey was very upset because his girlfriend had just told him she wanted to break up with him. She told him that she liked someone else better. Carey became angry, then acted out his anger by going home and punching the wall. What was transpiring inside Carey's mind as he drove to his apartment? Was he actually telling himself that if he hit the wall, he would feel better? No, he did not use those words. Instead, he acted on his inner subconscious beliefs.

Carey actually *believed* that hitting the wall was good for him—at least before he did it. He believed that the solution for relieving his discomfort was to act out his rage on something—by hitting or harming something. By believing this he hid the truth from himself. After he had calmed down, his hand required medical attention and the wall needed repairs. Before he hit the wall he did not tell himself such damage might result, though he certainly knew it. He also did not tell himself how his self-image would be considerably lessened by such behavior. He did not tell himself the truth that he would degrade himself by acting childishly and being out of control.

Carey had told himself a lie and hidden the truth from himself, in the same manner as we all do when we sin. Later, with two broken fingers, Carey told himself the truth: "Hitting walls doesn't make me feel better when I am upset." Though at the time of his outburst he did not actually say aloud, "Where can I find a nice wall to punch because that's going to make me feel real good," he *believed* such nonsense to be true. Mental pictures and feelings developed by past experience and observation contributed to his beliefs.

When we believe lies and repeat them over and over to ourselves, we help and enable ourselves to sin. The power of truth can end forever the misbelief to which we have so tenaciously clung, which tells us our bad behavior, which God has forbidden, is good for us.

A Sin by Any Other Name . . .

We all want to lead blessed, happy lives, but what can destroy us faster than a speeding bullet? Sin. God speaks of sin as three things: (1) an acquired or developed common human trait; (2) individual rebellious acts; (3) the power of Satan (the father of lies) and his demons. We can combat sin when we understand it is always accompanied by a lie.

Individual sins develop from accepting lies such as, "I must have _____," "I can't do without _____," "_____ is good for me." (It's not good for us at all. A good example is Carey's behavior; his broken fingers prove it.)

Most of us, when we think of sin, think of an individual act, a specific transgression, or a habitual behavior. However, in order to understand ourselves and the problems we find ourselves in, we must consider the deeper, radical nature of sin—the word "radical" refers to the root. According to the Scriptures, sin is not just individual or circumscribed actions; it is something which gets "under our skin," and becomes entwined in our very nature. We all then become sinners as we practice sin. The Lutheran Confessions describe sinners as ". . . without fear of God, . . . without trust in God, and . . . concupiscent" (*Augsburg Confession* II, 1). Not trusting

God is the act of the person in rebellion against the Creator.

"Concupiscence" means the disposition of man to believe the senses, the lies of the devil, and therefore deny and despise God and His truth. Concupiscence describes the deep inner willingness of man to believe the lie. From the very beginning sin has been the result of a lie.

Many people believe that we just sin and that's all there is to it. You may shrug and say, "I'm just a sinner and I can't help myself." *But you can help yourself.* There is a psychological dynamic underlying sinful behavior. By changing your thinking (an act of the will), you can change your behavior. Sometimes you may want to close the door on solutions that require some hard word on your part. You may prefer to sit back and wait for God to push some miraculous "holy" button within you, then, *presto*, all your troubles will be over. This will never happen. Every morning when you wake up, you will still be you with the same behaviors, good or bad, that you exhibited the day before. Unless you've done something about them.

The Scriptures tell us to *examine* ourselves in order to reach our fullest potential as Christians. It may not always be pleasant to talk about sin, but we need diagnosis before treatment. Without accurate diagnosis we will not know how to treat the malady. Each problem requires exacting treatment. Imagine a doctor prescribing aspirin for every physical symptom. What effect would this have on appendicitis?

The core truth on which our mental and emotional health and spiritual success depend is that sin is the problem, and Jesus Christ (who calls himself *the* truth) is the cure. The Holy Spirit, the spirit of truth, guides us into all truth. He teaches us through the Word to remove the lies that entrap us.

God is the ultimate psychologist and He has laid out foolproof guidelines for our mental well-being. As you work through this book, you will discover the correlation between your misbeliefs and sinful and neurotic behavior in your life. You will see how sin and neurotic behavior are closely related. This relationship exists because they each result from *misbelief.*

Misbelief Therapy

We have seen many lives set free from a multitude of besetting problems through what we call "Misbelief Therapy." Misbelief, as we describe it in our book *Telling Yourself the Truth,* * is the direct cause of emotional turmoil, maladaptive behavior and most so-called "mental illness." Misbeliefs are the cause of the destructive behavior people persist in even when they are fully aware that it is harmful to them (e.g., overeating, smoking, lying, drunkenness, stealing or adultery). *Misbeliefs are lies we accept as truth.*

The principles in this book focus on a group of sins traditionally referred to as the "seven deadly sins." As you apply the principles, you will soon be able to recognize how each of these horrible traps, such as pride, envy and anger, can infect your life. You will learn what to do to free yourself from them. You will also learn how to deal with the accompa-

---

Telling Yourself the Truth, Bethany House Publishers, Minneapolis, Minnesota, 1980.

nying emotional patterns which are as destructive as the sins themselves.

You will discover, for example, how living for others' approval is a neurotic response accompanying the sin of *pride*. You will learn to recognize the agonizing daily strife, anxiety and conflict with people which are generated by the sin of *envy*. You can know true liberation when you see that the lies accompanying the sins of pride, envy, anger, greed, sloth, lust and gluttony are based on what you tell yourself is *good* for you.

The problem? You, as all people, make mistakes. But Jesus, by His work on the cross, grants you the privilege of a life not dominated by sin. He is inviting you into a new way of life, one you perhaps have never before imagined possible.

CHAPTER THREE

God, Make Me Willing

"For the good that I wish, I do not do; but I practice the very evil that I do not wish" (Rom. 7:19, NASB).

If I speak a bad word or punch somebody in the nose, that is sin. If I steal someone's wallet or tell a lie, that is sin. These are individual acts of sin, which we spoke of in Chapter Two. Such commandments as "Thou shalt not steal," "Thou shalt not commit adultery," "Thou shalt not take the name of the Lord thy God in vain" are familiar to us.

Sin as a Human Trait

The Bible defines sin not only as an individual act, but as a universally developed human trait. A trait isn't something we do; a trait is not one specific

27

act. A trait is a disposition, something that influences our behavior. By repeatedly consenting to sin, we have developed this trait, this sinful nature. It means there is a higher-than-average probability that we will behave in a certain way—we will sin.

Our prayers become: "God make me willing to face my sin," and "God make me willing to give up my sins."

Here are some traits you may identify with: dependency, immorality, brashness, passivity, aggressiveness, anger. These aren't individual acts; they are characteristics. If we say Bella is a passive person, we mean that Bella most probably will do very little to alter her circumstances. If we say Arnold is a dependent person, we mean that something within him influences his behavior so that he clings to and depends upon significant people in his life.

For many centuries Christians were taught to recognize the seven deadly sins. They are:

Pride

Envy

Anger

Greed

Sloth

Lust

Gluttony

The concept of the seven deadly sins was taught to every man, woman and child to help them examine their behavior before God.

The seven deadly sins are *traits*, not *acts*. When we say Marvin has a lot of pride, we mean that what he does will be influenced by that pride. He'll talk a lot about himself, he'll want to run things, he'll be boastful and he won't want anybody telling him what to do.

Sin, as we will discuss it, is an inner dynamic. "But now being made free from sin, and become servants to God, ye had your fruit unto holiness, and the end everlasting life" (Rom. 6:22). Sin is something only humans have. Tigers, birds, or frogs don't have it. It is the single universal trait that saturates every wrong thing we do. We need a Savior!

What does sin do? It defies the commandments of God. God told Eve not to eat of the fruit of the knowledge of good and evil but the devil convinced Eve it would be good for her to try it. He told her she would then be as wise as God. So Eve ate the fruit. Sin attempted to defy, destroy, and exalt itself over God's righteous command. *The devil is only interested in promoting behavior which God forbids.*

Sin depends upon and grows out of the believing of certain lies. The genesis of sin is untruth. The genesis of neuroses is also untruth. It is the root of drunkenness as well as depression, the root of stealing as well as overeating.

There are two very common lies with which you may be familiar. The first is *"X" is good for me.* Sin results from the misbelief that something contrary to the Word of God is good for you. "X" can be stealing from a department store ("I deserve to have . . ."); or hitting the kid next door ("I can't control myself"); or skipping school when you're not supposed to ("It's good for me to do exactly as I please"); or lying to your wife ("I must be right. I must please people at all times"); or innumerable other sins. Sin may seem like something good for you because it will pamper you in some way, make you feel good, save you from trouble or embarrassment, flatter you or promote you. If it promotes you, how can God say it isn't good for you? Certainly God must not understand how tough things are for you.

Possibly you tell yourself a particular sin is good for you because you "need" it in your life—you can't do without it, it is fundamental to your happiness. So you steal that record from the record department, you lie on your time sheet at work or cheat on your income tax because you believe "it's good for me."

The second common untruth is, *I can't help myself.* This sin says, "I've got to do it. I am helpless to stop myself. The temptation is bigger than I am." How many times have you forsaken your diet and eaten some fattening mess even though you knew you shouldn't because you said, "Oh, I just can't help myself"? Some people have given up and started smoking again because they have told themselves, "I can't make it. I'm too weak to be able to quit cigarettes." Some people have even committed adultery believing the same kind of lie.

So "X" looks good for today. You're only human, after all. And you just don't have any resistance; surely God can understand that. (You really don't *want* resistance because you'd rather believe "X" is good for you.)

This is how sin deceives. And according to Romans 7, sin kills. "X" is *not* good for you. "X" is lethal. It kills. Jesus met "X" with the truth. The devil came to Him and said, "Making bread out of stones is good for you. It will prove you're the Son of God. No one will doubt you after that." Satan also tried to convince Jesus that jumping off the temple's pinnacle was good for Him. He told Him, "It will prove to the people you really are the Messiah. What can it hurt? It will be good for you because then I'll give you the kingdom without the cross."

Jesus met every temptation by challenging its accompanying lie. He said in effect, "That isn't true, Satan. The truth is, thou shalt not tempt the Lord thy God." Jesus demonstrated by His example that we should live only by the words that proceed out of the mouth of God. We can take the first step toward defeating temptation by refusing to put ourselves into a place where we listen to Satan's lies.

God has provided the ultimate solution: the lamb of God, as the sacrifice of God, bore every one of our "X's" in His body on the cross. By dying on the cross, He became our righteousness, our sanity. We now can be righteous and have the power of overcoming sin through Jesus Christ. God obliterates our sins in the blood of the Lamb. In the blood of Jesus there is tremendous power. Not just power to wash a blackboard with our past sins written all over it, but power to keep us from future sins.

When it comes to living the Christian life, we put our lives where our heads are, so to speak. What we *believe* is what we will do. The fellow who lights a cigarette and smokes it, despite the warnings of the Surgeon General's report, believes that it is more important to inhale his pleasure today than to be healthy tomorrow. He may wholly agree with what the Surgeon General prints on the package, but he lights up anyway. If he believed that he would drop dead instantly from that very cigarette, would he light it? If you were to stand beside him with a gun aimed at his temple and tell him if he smoked that cigarette you would pull the trigger, chances are he wouldn't do it. He would show some self-control. But right now nothing stops him and he tells himself the lie, "One more won't hurt me."

Many Bible heroes of the past made mistakes that

did irreparable damage. Their examples now help and instruct us because we not only learn from triumphs, but from failures. The culprit in the lives of famous Bible characters is the same as for you and me: misbelief.

SOME FAMOUS BIBLE PEOPLE AND THEIR MISBELIEFS

David the King

The challenge to hide our sins from ourselves as well as from others is always a temptation. Remember David and Bathsheba? It was David's cover-up and refusal to face his sin that added coals to the fire of his already terrible deeds involving Bathsheba and her husband. Adultery led to murder, and more death and misery resulted.

How did it begin? David watched Bathsheba bathing on her porch and must have said to himself, "It would be good to take her from her husband." He excused his sin of lust. Do you see the lie? Whom was he kidding? He was headed for disaster!

David probably continued by telling himself the following lies: "I'm king, after all, so I have special privileges that no one else has. What difference does it make that Bathsheba is already married? I'm the king, I'm supposed to get what I want, and what I want is more important than what anybody else wants. Because I *want* it, it must be good."

What David wanted was *not* good. Eventually he paid dearly for his sin and other people also suffered. Several died, including the child of their adultery. David and Bathsheba believed the things that adulterers always believe. The major lie in this sin is,

"Adultery may usually be wrong, but in our case, it's so wonderful and so beautiful that it *must* be all right." St. Augustine said he had a very difficult time dealing with adulterers because he found it hard to convince them that their affair, which they saw as lovely and noble, was not right, that it was *sin*. Another lie of adultery is, "I can't help it." David was so entranced with Bathsheba that he just "couldn't help it."

An adulterer must tell himself a host of lies like David's in order to sin. Even if he can't recognize the lies right away, they are there.

Achan the Thief

The army of Israel had experienced a mighty victory against Jericho, but God had made very clear that they were not to take any spoils from their conquered foe. Achan, however, did not obey. He must have told himself, "The enemy's spoils are good for me. I can't just destroy them. That would be a terrible waste. In the face of my family's need, why destroy all these goods?" His final misbelief may have been to tell himself the fault for stealing would not be his. "This law is probably just one of Moses' legalistic threats." He assumed no one would know if he took just a few things that didn't belong to him.

A dominant misbelief in greed is, "I can't trust God to supply. I must hoard up goods for myself because every man is on his own." What Achan thought would be good for him was not. He believed a lie. Because he disobeyed the law many Israelite soldiers died, and Achan, his wife and children were stoned to death.

Joseph's Jealous Brothers

When Joseph was young his brothers felt they had a right to be upset with him. They believed, "It's terrible to think that Joseph is better than we are" (the sin of envy). They believed they could not tolerate his being their father's favorite. They believed it was unfair, outrageous, terrible. They were ready for the next lie: "It is all right to get rid of him."

Samson the Nazarite

Talk about physical fitness! Samson never worked out in a gym or health spa, yet he was the strongest man on earth. In spite of all his physical accomplishments, his belief system was a mess. What caused him to violate his Nazarite vows? to throw away the wonderful gifts God had given him? If you had been Samson's pastor, what would you have told him? How about, "Samson, when are you going to believe some truth?"

Here is what Samson must have believed when he met Delilah: "It's much more important that I please Delilah than to keep these Nazarite vows which are insignificant now in the face of love. To have Delilah's acceptance will be good for me. It will make me happy." The whole nation of Israel suffered because of Samson's misbeliefs. The lie he believed, "Pleasing Delilah will be good for me," brought him only pain. His eyes were gouged out and he spent his final days grinding grain like an animal before his death.

Ahab the Wicked King

Ahab hated the word "no." He saw a little vineyard next to his palace and asked Naboth, the owner, to sell it to him. Naboth refused. Ahab became so upset he would not eat. He just lay on his bed and sulked (no way for a king to behave). What do you suppose Ahab was doing as he lay sulking? Telling himself lies.

Though largely unspoken, here's what he believed: "I *must* have that vineyard. I can't eat unless I have that vineyard. It's awful that Naboth won't part with it. If I don't have that vineyard, I just won't ever get off this bed. It's outrageous I can't have what I want. I should *always* get everything I want. I can't be happy unless I get what I want."

He got what he wanted, all right, through the aid of his wicked wife, Jezebel. While Ahab lay brooding in his room, Jezebel devised a plan and had Naboth murdered. Her husband got the vineyard he wanted.

Was Ahab believing the truth when he said the vineyard would be good for him? For assenting to evil, he met destruction on every corner. He was killed in battle and Jezebel was thrown out of a window and devoured by dogs.

Pilate the Weak-Kneed Governor

Pilate believed it was more important to please people than to carry out justice. He believed it would be safer for him and his position if he unjustly approved the crucifixion of Jesus in order to please the crowd. Society's approval was so vital to him, it was worth everything—even the life of the Savior of the world.

When you sin, do you actually ask yourself, "How will I have to pay for this sin?" Chances are you don't believe you'll have to pay for whatever it is you're about to do. You may instead tell yourself, "I need to do this. I am out of control. God won't punish me for being out of control." Sin has consequences, though, and it's important to recognize that truth. Jesus forgives us for sin, but the lie above will keep you from receiving it.

How Others View Sin

The *evolutionist* sees sin as immaturity and imperfection. The necessary process to eliminate sin is viewed as simply further evolutionary progress.

The *genetic technologist* may view sin as nothing more than undesirable behavior which can eventually be bred out of the human race. A behavioral geneticist told a conference of theologians, "Tell us what behaviors you define as sin and we will eliminate them from the gene pool so that what you call sin will no longer exist."

The *humanist* teaches that imperfection is not catastrophic, and that nothing—including the worst of sins—is really bad. One can always tell himself, "So what? I'm not perfect." Here's the catch: In humanism, man is the final authority. All that stands in the way of what he wants (including morality) must go. Humanism says there are no absolutes, no rights, no wrongs—moral values are self-determined and situational. It denies the existence of a personal God, the inspiration of the Bible, and the divinity of Jesus Christ.

Holistic philosophy sees man as deity. Stephen Gasken, Haight-Ashbury's acid guru, speaking for the counterculture of holistic medicine and pantheistic religion which promotes the old notion, "You are all gods" says, "We believe that everybody is basically good. We are all perfect when we're born and pick up bad habits as we go along." Gasken says, "Once you understand the unsulliable [sic] nature of the intellect, it's no longer necessary to seek absolution for past sins." He claims anyone who understands this can be absolved in the here and now.*

Christian Scientists believe there is no devil, no evil, and therefore no sin. This cult, and other similar ones, teach that it is our choice to succeed or fail as we climb life's ladder because everything around us is positive. We need only connect our consciousness to the all-in-all of God. This rules out all individuality, all material reality, all evil, all sickness, indeed *all*. For, if God is all, all is nothing but God.

According to this belief, evil is an illusion. Sin and disease are figments of the mortal mind. There is no need of a Savior because there is nothing to be saved from. Mary Baker Eddy, the originator of Christian Science, once wrote to her friend and disciple, Judge Hanna, "I have marvelled at the press's and pulpit's patience with me when I have taken away their Lord."*

We can find thousands of secular books at the bookstores promising us ways to be happy with futile and useless methods. Most of the books contain non-Christian, humanistic teachings which focus on technique—"How to Do It." Transcendental meditation is a technique. Drugs are a technique. Existentialism, such as the philosophy of Jean Paul Sartre, is a technique of self-authentication. The "Zeitgeist," the humanistic, anti-theistic, monistic are all just techniques. And they miss the mark.

---

*"Hey Beatnik!" *SEPC Journal,* Vol. 4–1 (April, 1981), 20.

*John H. Gerstner, *The Teachings of Christian Science,* Grand Rapids, Michigan: Baker Book House, 1981.

Sin Makes Us Neurotic

The everyday lives of the above Bible characters
reflected their sin as well as God's acts of judgment.
Achan was sneaky; Samson was impetuous; Jezebel
was a hostile and venomous woman; Pilate was
spineless. David, during his cover-up, was no picture
of emotional well-being. He was a nervous wreck,
sleepless and constantly worried. Scripture shows
David far more distraught over his unconfessed sin
than he was over Saul's murderous pursuit during
his younger years. At least when running from Saul,
David knew that God was with him.

Consider Adam and Eve. They behaved most ab-
normally after they had sinned. They ran about in
fear, hiding behind bushes, covering their bodies with
leaves. They lied, blamed each other for their problems, and shrank from the very One who had given
them life and loved them. Was it normal for them to
hide from someone they loved and who loved them?
No, they had lost sight of the truth.

Sin is no fun when seen for what it is. To put it
bluntly, it makes us crazy. It robs us of inner peace.

The Right Kind of Faith

Let's invent a new word—orthopistis. *Ortho*
means straight, right, correct. *Pistis* is belief, faith.
The word orthopistis would mean right faith. That
is what we need to overcome any sin.

How do we become orthopistists? By acquiring
faith. We know that "faith cometh by hearing and
hearing by the word of God" (Rom. 10:17). To hear
Him is to hear the voice of triumph and holiness.

One thing we learn to do as orthopistists is not to

make up God's mind for Him and then believe what we have decided is true. We cannot put words in His mouth and try to run our own show. Orthopistis is a reaction to the Word: (1) We receive the Word. (2) We believe the Word. (3) We do something about it.

Suppose your friend has said he can't help you with an important job as he promised he would. You're furious; your feelings are hurt. You're thinking, *How could he do this to me? He had promised to help.* As an orthopistist (ortho means *straight*), you are going to want to make this situation straight. Instead of blasting your friend in anger, or saying nothing at all (which could be more punishing than blasting him), you could do something like the following:

- Speak to yourself about your own feelings. "I feel angry and hurt" would be an honest appraisal.
- Objectively analyze the situation. "In spite of my feelings, this situation is not as bad as the Chicago Fire or World War III. I can handle it."

In the past, when you were mad at somebody, maybe you fantasized an act of revenge. After nurturing the anger, you may have acted out what you told yourself should be done. Did you experience a sense of release? No. You probably felt guilty instead.

When you are studying the Word of God, get it *straight*. (Ortho means straight.) You are to get straight what God says in His Word. Then when you are in a difficult situation, ask yourself three questions: (1) What am I telling myself about this situation? (2)What does *God* say about the situation? (3)

Do I agree with what God says?

You will know what God says if you have been studying it, hearing it in church and meditating on it. So then you must ask yourself, do I *agree* with it?

The Word tells you, "I can do *all* things through Christ which strengtheneth me" (Phil. 4:13). The Word tells you that if friends and family forsake you, He will never leave you. Admit, "Yes, Lord. I receive those words as truth. Your Word is truth. I will accept your Word with all my heart and soul."

Then *trust* the Word. Even though your friend abandoned you when you needed him, The Word of God is present to rescue you.

When you believe what God says in His Word is true and workable, you can act on it. This is how you overcome sin. You act on the Word of God because you know it; you accept it as truth and trust it.

"Easier said than done," you say. Yes, sometimes you may feel compelled to argue with God. Sometimes you may actually get mad at God. (But you don't tell anyone, of course. Instead you mistreat yourself and everyone around you.) You tell God by your actions, "How come you haven't made me rich like you said you would?" or "How come you haven't corrected this loneliness in my life?" or "Why haven't you given me a job yet?" or "How come you haven't healed me yet?" If something is wrong the problem must be God. It couldn't be *you*—could it?

The problem, most likely, is your beliefs. You know what God says and yet you argue with Him and tell yourself, "But I'm only human—I've got my needs. I can't live like a monk or nun. I must have these diversions once in a while. God made me with these needs, so He should understand." You're certain that *you* know what is good for you. God doesn't.

How can you be an orthopistist? How can you have the right belief? Right belief comes about when you honestly and openly face the wrong beliefs you have allowed to fester in your mind, and when you choose to act on the truth.

Pray now:

Father, because Jesus rose from the dead I can face the lies I have allowed to go unchallenged in my life. I choose to overcome sin in my life. I give you permission to be Lord of every belief, thought, idea, dream, goal and desire I have. I will believe and act on the truth because You are truth and truth dwells in me. In Jesus' name. Amen.

CHAPTER FOUR

What Egoes Up Usually Comes Down

The Pride of Superiority

Picture in your mind Cassie, a sweet-looking lady with a soft voice and quiet manner. She involves herself in several church activities, and her unassuming presence is barely noticeable. Cassie would never seek out someone, assertively introduce herself and start a conversation. Though she attends church every week faithfully, she has no friends she considers close to her. She lives her life quietly and alone and considers herself "humble." She gives the impression of being inoffensive and yes, humble.

But Cassie isn't what she seems. The deadly sin of pride is being manifested in her as the *pride of superiority*. Cassie does not seem depressed, anxious, tense, or upset. However, she has sought counseling because her pastor suggested it might help her frequent headaches. Her therapist concluded Cassie was experiencing feelings of persecution, alienation and isolation.

Cassie's life is terribly constricted; she is friendless, lonely, and because of the pride of superiority, feels persecuted. She worries that people will hurt her, that they will turn on her because she is nearly perfect and therefore superior to them. Such pride can be deadly because underneath the aura of superiority Cassie strives helplessly to counteract feelings of low self-confidence.

What conflict! Cassie is covering up shyness, nervousness and low self-esteem with a superior attitude. Many people do this, telling themselves they are superior to others and that within them is an element of greatness nobody else has. This is usually carried out through silent, unrecognized self-talk.

A person with the pride of superiority is easy prey to flattery, although he or she will not actually believe the flattery. Inwardly he suspects the flatterer is misinformed or else manipulating him for some favor.

Cassie had a chain of misbeliefs in the following areas of her life:

Community Life: "I am a Christian person and God loves me just as I am, which is morally better than most of the people around me."

Work Life: "My supervisor and employer are criticizing my work because they realize that I am better than they are. Because I am better, I stand a chance of losing my job. The boss is jealous of me."

Home Life: "If only my family could see the light

and do things God's way" (actually this means, *my* way).

We create our own tensions. The world around us may be full of turmoil and strife, but we can decide not to accept the lies and allow them to dictate our emotions and behaviors.

Superiority pride says, "I must try even harder to be perfect so that nobody will ever find fault with me. I must be very, very humble so people won't consider me pushy. I must do flawless work. Other people are persecuting me in every way they can, so I must be spotless and perfect, no matter what." Such thinking causes so much tension that job performance is impaired, and of course, the personality is impaired to such a degree that friends and family think they are being rejected (paranoia and withdrawal causes others to believe they are not matching up to expectations). In a way they are right because in the case of Cassie, she wants to believe that she is superior to others. Her present condition is built on the lie that she is perfect and the rest of the world is responsible for her troubles.

An act such as curling the lip toward someone or finding fault with another person may indicate the pride of superiority. Most people with this pride do not outwardly appear to be judgmental or hateful. But inwardly, because of their need for relief from self-loathing, pride is a defense.

The pride of superiority is a comfort. Have you ever heard something like this? "Look at that dumb so-and-so driving down the freeway! Did you see what a *stupid* thing he did?"

The pride of superiority shows itself in many ways. Anger toward God is the most flagrant of all. Jonah's story is a good example of this.

Jonah's Pride

Jonah's pride of superiority over the Ninevites exposed the lies he was believing. Even though Jonah wanted to run away from God, God said in effect, "Jonah, I'm going to use you. It would be so much better for all of us if you would believe the *truth* and employ a cheerful, compassionate heart as you perform the task I've called you to do."

Jonah, with his superior attitude, questioned God's wisdom. He couldn't see why God wanted to save the Ninevites. He had been called by God to bring a nation spiritual revival, but he considered himself too good for them. He had his reasons, of course. After all, the Ninevites were merciless and ravagers of his country, and Jonah was a partisan as well as a patriot. He wanted God to destroy Nineveh, certainly not save it. Jonah demonstrated the pride of superiority by his avoidance behavior. He sulked, complained, brooded and refused to hear the truth.

Cassie and Jonah believed the same lies. They believed they had the right to sin. Frightened and alienated from others, they believed their sin was justifiable. Cassie believed humility is good. She therefore gave the outward impression of humility (which she considered a good thing to do) and thus felt herself superior to others. Jonah believed he was superior to the Ninevites. Because he was a Jew and not one of them, he believed he was more perfect than they.

The Pride of Suffering

A man and wife are without jobs and living on very meager means. They believe they are suffering more than most people. They believe that being poor makes them humble and godly. They pooh-hooh the rich and especially find fault with Christians who have money or live well. This exhibition of the pride of suffering is due to their belief that their own suffering is something holy and good while the prosperity of others is suspect and even ungodly.

"Only *I* know what living for God really means" is the lie. "My suffering gives me a higher rank in the eyes of God. Others have many problems, but only I really know what overcoming is all about." The progression of lies is: It is humbling and godly to suffer. I am suffering. Therefore, I am more humble and godly than those who are not suffering.

See what nonsense such logic is? Anything that makes you feel superior to others is not humbling. Being poor cannot make you spiritually more rich than others. Being poor is no virtue in itself. Neither is suffering something to wave a flag for nor bow the knee to. A person degrades himself *and* the Lord if he tells himself such lies as, "By remaining unemployed and not knowing where the next meal is coming from, I'm earning favor from God."

Humility is not self-degradation. When you degrade yourself you are acting in pride. Humility is to love others and feel good about yourself at the same time. A good response against temptation to this kind of pride would be, "I am not better than anyone else because of suffering or not suffering. No one else is better than I either. I choose to be humble God's way and not mine."

The Apostle Peter wept tears of anguish and despair after he had denied Jesus. At the moment of denying the Lord, his behavior said, "Right now my life is more important than anything in the world. I am superior to these negative events and do not want to be dragged down by this humiliating trial." Later, as Peter sobbed bitterly over his plight, he no doubt felt his life had hit bottom in the pit of worthlessness. What was Jesus' response? He not only restored Peter to fellowship, He made him the spokesman at Pentecost, and a mighty minister of God whose influence is still touching the world. He was a humble man, a fisherman; yet his words penned in Scripture live as an eternal reminder of the mercy and power of God.

Nobody is superior to anybody else. Nobody is less important than anybody else, no matter what station of life we are in.

The Pride of Other-Control

Billy sticks out his chin and says defiantly, "Don't tell *me* what to do." He is firmly standing his ground, clearly a person of decisiveness and willpower. He knows what he wants in life and nobody's going to take it from him. He certainly can run things better than anyone else. One problem: Billy is the only one who thinks so.

Self-control, a fruit of the Holy Spirit, is not Billy's forte. He strives for *other*-control. The pride of other-control is the inability to tolerate a situation unless in charge of it. The basic lies Billy has nurtured are: (1) My life shouldn't be subject to the orders of anybody else; and (2) I should be the one to decide what other people do; and (3) I can do things just as well if not better than other people so they have no right to make demands of me.

Billy will deny that he makes demands to control others. If confronted, he will exclaim, "Who me? I

certainly am not trying to control anyone. I'm perfectly happy to allow other people to be in the driver's
seat. The reason I have to make all the decisions is
because nobody else does."

The pride of other-control will surface in anger
when somebody else has the authority. If you don't
like to be told what to do by your pastor, your spouse,
your teachers, or your parents, you might suspect a
drive to control people. Do you find fault with fellow
Christians? Do you resent law-enforcement officers?
Some people get angry just at the sight of a police-
man on the street because he represents a greater
authority.

The person who feels he or she must be in charge
at all times and in all situations devalues others'
positions of authority: "All cops are crooks," "All doctors are quacks," "The president is a jerk. . . ." The
lie in the pride of other-control is, "I have every right
to feel the way I do."

The Pride of Vanity

The pride of vanity is rooted in the misbelief, "The
most important thing in life is that other people think
highly of me and have only good and positive opinions of me." Note, please, there is no sin in receiving
human attention or having others speak well of you.
A problem surfaces when you believe you've *got* to
have attention, when you can't endure not being appreciated or recognized.

Following close behind the initial misbelief of the
pride of vanity are these two lies: *"I can't stand it if
I am not noticed,"* and, *"I can't stand it if, when I am
noticed, somebody doesn't think well of me."*

The pride of vanity craves attention. A person

with the pride of vanity finds it difficult to pass the mirror without looking and adjusting his appearance. The pride of vanity uses the pronoun "I" often. Such a person brags and boasts and will subtly or unsubtly advertise how wonderful he is. For instance, a woman with the pride of vanity may tell you how handsome, talented, brilliant, and marvelous her husband and/or her children are. She sometimes will boast and brag to the point of being obnoxious, all the while thinking she is simply being supportive and encouraging to her loved ones, but actually swelling her own ego. The pride of vanity is never satisfied with anything less than the greatest, the biggest and the best. The person with the pride of vanity feels he must be part of something earth-shaking in order to be assured he is impressing others.

You may be saying now, "I don't have the pride of vanity because I never boast. In fact, whenever I talk about myself I put myself down. I always try to lift other people up higher than I."

Mary, a woman of thirty-nine, said, "Whenever I have people over for dinner and my guests tell me how much they have enjoyed the meal, I always tell them, 'Well, I think I could have done better,' or I'll say, 'I suppose I could have cooked beef instead of chicken,' or something like that. I always manage to put myself down so that no one will think I'm proud."

That may sound like a person who is not vain, but that assumption is wrong. The person who puts himself or herself down as Mary does is really trying very hard to get someone else to say, "Why, you're wonderful." The only way to obtain such reassurance is to put yourself down so others will argue and tell you how terrific you are. That is the pride of vanity.

When we sin we are telling ourselves that something is good for us even if God has told us clearly it is not good. Even as Christians we can be misled to think that we and what we do are the most important things in the world—rather than God and His doings. Pride says things like, "I have to prove myself to be perfect. I must be 100% committed to my endeavors, and if I am only 99% successful, that is not good enough. I must try harder. I must work harder. I must improve, advance, achieve and do something of value, or die."

Now I ask you, is this the kind of person you want as a friend, husband, wife, boss, sister, or brother? Such a person tells God, "Watch me improve myself without your help. Watch me get more spiritual." The proud person loses sight of the fact that the only way to improve, advance, achieve, and grow spiritually is through Christ and through the guidance of His Spirit of Truth.

The Pride of Presumption

Presumptuous pride says, "I can do anything. In fact, I can do anything better than you can." We see a lot of this kind of pride in people who believe they are qualified to give medical advice without medical training. Presumption is the belief that anything anybody else does I can do also. Even if I clearly don't have the ability, I behave as if I did. The pride of presumptuousness believes these lies: (1) "I should have all the authority and ability anybody else does, spiritual or otherwise." (2) "It's intolerable that somebody should be higher than I. I ought to be the teacher or the preacher or the one in charge or the one getting all the recognition." (3) "I can do a better

job than the other person, even without preparing."
(4) "It's intolerable that other people get to do things
I am denied. I should be able to try everything."

The person with the pride of presumption will
think he can order God around. This person will decide what he or she wants and then believe that he
can have it and tell God, "I expect you to do exactly
as I say." The pride of presumption actually lowers
God; it orders Him around and uses scripture to back
up the presumptuousness.

The Pride of Rebellion

If a person with the pride of rebellion thinks
someone is telling him or her what to do, he becomes
most upset. He hates criticism. A rebellious person
will not allow anyone to tell him there is anything
wrong with him. When the pride of rebellion holds a
ruling position in a life, the person will reveal in a
number of ways that he is saying to God, "Move over,
God. You have been hogging the throne too long. It's
not right that I, with all my abilities and potential,
should be restrained from power." He or she may
even get angry and have a temper tantrum.

The pride of rebellion is revealed when we insist
we do something no matter what anybody else says
about it. Suppose I decide that I intend to steal something. Before I do it, I will have to tell God to move
over—"Quit running my life, God, because if you run
my life I can't steal." Of course, I would never actually say those words or form such a sentence because I don't admit to myself I have those feelings.

Suppose you become angry at your wife because
you're tired of being sweet and understanding when
she treats you so badly. For once you're going to really

let her have it. You think you have a right to tell God to move over because He's been running your life all wrong. After all, your wife is just getting increasingly arrogant.

Name a sin that is a problem for you and it will be a sin you think you have every right to commit. Whenever you sin you have to believe something is good for you which God has said is not good. The pride of rebellion says it's good to get your own way no matter who you hurt or how you get it.

The Pride of Denial

Connie and Joe are seated together on the sofa in the counseling office. Connie is huddled on the edge of the cushion of her chair, her face showing obvious distress. Her hands in her lap are twisted together, fingers digging into her palms. Joe sits placidly, his face expressionless except for a slight, tolerant smile. His arms are folded across his chest. His eyes avert the therapist's as well as his wife's.

Connie's voice quivers with emotion: "I can't stand it. I just want out of the marriage. I've never loved Joe. I didn't love him when we were married and I don't love him now." Then to her husband she says tightly, "Please understand, it has nothing to do with you, Joe. I feel we're just plain incompatible."

After a long silence, Joe says, "I believe God put this marriage together and I believe with some effort it could work out."

The therapist asks, "What do you mean, 'work out,' Joe?"

Joe recites a string of vague sentences beginning like this: "The Bible clearly teaches that divorce is a sin and that if there are no grounds for a divorce such as adultery, then it's wrong. I believe that God can help me and help our marriage, and if we work at it He will give my wife love in her heart for me."

The situation, as you can see, is serious. A wife is miserable and riddled with guilt and anguish because she does not love her husband and because she is afraid God is going to punish her horribly for wanting out. Her husband calmly and self-righteously says, "God will do something."

Joe is manifesting pride of denial when he refuses to acknowledge his own failures and finds a convenient, religious-sounding speech to duck behind.

We can use God as an excuse, but God doesn't want that. Neither does He want to be used as a club to beat someone into submission. We must let God be God. The pride of denial refuses to admit there is anything wrong with us. "My marriage in trouble? Don't be silly. God will work it out and straighten out my mate." Why is it usually the *mate* who is at fault?

Joe would not tell his wife that he loved her deeply and wanted to make a beautiful life for her. He would not ask for her forgiveness. Instead, he told her what *God* had to say. He refused to see his own shortcomings that were contributing to the situation. He denied the truth in order to protect his pride. To deny his own inadequacies as well as the inadequacies of the marriage was as much sin as the inadequacies themselves.

In an effort to retaliate against Connie's lack of love for him, Joe deliberately withheld himself from her. He refused to give her that which she would have loved in him—the truth. He kept her in bondage to him by telling her she would practically be committing the unpardonable sin if she considered leaving the marriage. Joe would continue to deny his problems and Connie would continue to feel unloved and guilty.

The Pride of Passivity

Both Connie and Joe are guilty of pride. Neither is totally innocent. Connie gives the appearance of the pride of rebelliousness, but it would be more accurate to say she has the pride of *passivity*. She has passively accepted a life of misery, refusing to do anything constructive about it until it is too late.

We earlier discussed the pride of presumption—insisting one can do something he usually cannot. The pride of passivity, however, shows itself as *not* doing that which one is clearly able to do. Connie could have long ago confronted her husband openly and honestly, and then sought help. She claims she did tell him how unhappy she was, that she had told him so at least ten thousand times. She failed, though, to insure that Joe understood what she was saying. Because Joe would not acknowledge the problem, he really didn't believe her feelings were important. He ignored her expressions of unhappiness. So Connie did not pursue the matter. The lie Connie believed was, "It's right for me to hurt myself this way. It's good to do nothing when there is a problem at hand."

It can be difficult and even painful to admit the lies you have been telling yourself, to admit you really don't have the right to sin. That is why you tend to blame somebody or something else when wrong. Connie wanted to blame Joe for her misery and Joe wanted to blame God.

All of the sins of pride have at least one thing in

common: each is founded on lies. Each results from perversion of the truth.

The Pride of Self-sufficiency

Many times we treat God as just a good resource, someone to be consulted when things are too difficult to handle by ourselves. Don't think only non-Christians are guilty of this. We Christians may pray, read our Bibles and go to church, and yet never truly reach out for more and more of Jesus and give ourselves to a total dependence upon God. We aren't always the God-sufficient people we were called to be. When God is our sufficiency, we become completely dependent, for He—the all powerful one—is at the helm of our lives. It's a strange paradox that the more helpless we become toward Him, the stronger we become. This does not mean that we can sit back, do nothing and say, "If God wants me to go to church, He'll just have to wake me up and get me there." That's like saying, "If God wants me to breathe, He'll do it for me." God empowers us, but we must still choose to act.

The pride of self-sufficiency says, "I will get out of life just what I put into it," and "I can manage my own life," and "A person needs to learn to stand on his own two feet," and "When I was your age, I was already earning my own living!" All of these statements may *sound* reasonable, but pride turns good into evil. For example, the "I can manage my own life" misbelief means that all rewards must be self-directed and self-gratifying, even to the exclusion of God.

Don't be surprised when we tell you Christians can crave praise and attention just as anyone else. However, craving attention and *desiring* it are two different things. One gains attention when he stops craving it. Does that sound confusing? Connie craved attention. She was desperate for attention. When it did not come from her husband, she retreated into self-pity and told herself the only way she could get what she wanted was to leave her husband.

Pride not only craves attention but nearly goes mad without it. The pride of self-sufficiency will applaud itself, boast about itself and always do that which it thinks is best for itself. The pride of self-sufficiency will be found in the person who craves and seeks contacts with people who can help him or her. He also seeks out people who are pathetically needy or in distress so he can feel superior.

Here are some pride of superiority misbeliefs:

- "I'm so terrific I can tell others what to do."
- "I've got the answer and others don't."
- "I'm better than others because I'm more self-sufficient."
- "I'm important because others come to me for help."
- "People need someone like me because I have the answers and help they need."
- "People who are in need are inferior to me because I'm not in need."

The prideful act of being the superior one over the inferior one gives one the distinction of being able to talk about it. "Oh, poor Matilda. She's depressed again—just can't seem to get a grip on herself. She was here again to ask *me* for my counsel and advice. Naturally I helped as much as I could, and I told her to put her trust in the Lord. . . ."

The pride of self-sufficiency says, "People are helped when they come to me and I deserve a lot of praise for that." The person then can say such things as, "Oh, no, don't give me any praise. I just give all the glory to the Lord."

To be free of self-sufficient pride, we have to admit we have it. That is the first step toward deliverance. When we admit there is a problem we can be on the way to healing and renewal.

The symptoms of pride are unrest, inner conflict, frustration, rage, anxiety, depression and fear. Repentance is a major step to release from the agonies of pride. This brings us to the last category of pride: the pride of impenitence.

The Pride of Impenitence

The impenitent person finds it very difficult to admit a wrong or a mistake. It is painful to be wrong and have to feel the dreadful guilt and shame that result.

Jerry is a little boy of ten. His mother says to him, "You left the back door open again. How many times have I told you to close that door? Go and close it before I give you a spanking." Jerry, instead of saying, "I'm sorry for leaving the door open," exclaims, "I didn't do it! Tommy did it." Jerry has learned early that admitting the truth can be painful. He is learning that an apology is nonrewarding and even dangerous.

Picture Jerry at the dinner table. His father knocks over the gravy dish accidentally. A flutter of activity follows as his mother rushes to get something to clean up the gravy. Jerry's father, instead of apologizing for his accidental behavior, exclaims loudly, "Why did you leave that dish right there in my way? Look at what you've made me do!" He has shown Jerry that the way to handle a mistake is to avoid taking responsibility for it and not to ask forgiveness.

There are two major mistaken opinions of God that the impenitent person will have: *The first mistaken opinion* is, God is a horribly unfair law enforcer in the sky who is never satisfied with anything a person does. He is so perfect that no person can ever meet His demands. This misunderstanding pictures God as an irascible sort who is intensely difficult to get along with. The impenitent person believes that fairness means allowing him to do whatever he wants to do. It's only fair to get the rewards he demands without any interference. God is just a big bully.

The second mistaken opinion is, God is inept. He does not want His children making too much noise because He does not like to be disturbed. He likes people to do their own thing and call Him only on religious holidays, notable occasions and emergencies.

Both views are ridiculous. The almighty God of the universe is able to answer every one of our needs and to defeat our enemy who constantly fires *lies* at us. Only truth defeats the lie. But the impenitent person continues to believe the lie because he believes either that God would never accept his repentance or that He doesn't care. The reason impenitence is so tragic is that without repentance we can never have victory over sin.

A teenager told us about his bad temper. He had asked the Lord to help him overcome it, and told God, "I am really going to work on my temper. I'm going to try harder. Next time I'm going to try to be nice instead of blowing up." The following week the young man returned to our office in a cloud of discouragement. "I tried to control my temper but I couldn't. I'm a total failure. I pray and make resolutions but nothing ever happens." He had not yet repented.

What keeps us from telling God we are *sorry*? Sometimes we envision repentance as an emotional wrenching, feeling very awful about our sins. We think that the more horrible we feel about what we've done wrong, the more pleased God will be with us. So we cry and cry and try to feel as terrible as we can about our sins so God will feel sympathetic and forgive and help us. This is not what the Scriptures say.

Repentance does not mean to beat our breast wildly and frantically in despair and saturate our minds with downgrading thoughts and feelings about ourselves. The Greek word for repentance is *metanoiete*. This word means to change our mind. This does not mean to order a hamburger and five minutes later change the order to a tuna sandwich. *Metanoiete* means to exchange our old mind for a new one. The mind that is full of lies, full of deceit and blindfolded to righteousness, will never be free.

There is no sin too big to overcome. There may be some defeats, but the defeats must not be illogically thought of as failure. The words, "I will never get this sin out of my life," are not true.

It is hard to say the words "I'm sorry" when we are angry and telling ourself lies such as, "I never get what I want." It's those lying thoughts in the mind which need to be confronted and removed.

A new mind full of the truth is able to say, "Forgive me, Lord. I've believed lies." The motive of sin is deicide, or literally, God-murder. Sin wants to take away God's good and glory—to "ungod" God. *Truth* and repentance are the keys to freedom.

What happens when we repent? What happens when we turn to God as Job did and tell Him honestly, "Wherefore I abhor myself, and repent in dust and ashes" (Job 42:6)? What happens when we return to the Father as the prodigal son did? The prodigal son said to his father, "I have sinned against heaven, and in thy sight, and am no more worthy to be called thy son" (Luke 15:21). Both of these men had believed lies in order to sin as they did. Job had been guilty of a type of self-sufficiency—"Therefore have I uttered that I understood not; things too wonderful for me which I knew not" (Job 42:3). The prodigal son had believed the lies of the pride of rebellion: "Nobody can tell *me* what to do." We sin because we convince ourselves we have a right to defy the will of God.

When Job saw the truth and repented, God blessed him beyond his dreams.

The prodigal son realized the truth and returned home with a broken heart. He begged forgiveness of his father who then killed the fatted calf for a feast, gave him his ring, dressed him in fine clothes and threw a lavish banquet in celebration, restoring him as heir.

> *How precious is Thy lovingkindness, O God!*
> *And the children of men take refuge in the shadow of thy wings.*
> *They drink their fill of the abundance of Thy house;*
> *And Thou dost give them to drink of the river of Thy delights.*
> *For with Thee is the fountain of life;*
> *In Thy light we see light*
>   (Psalm 36:7–9, NASB).

We must refuse the lies that say, "Move over God, I'm taking charge now," or "I *must have. . . .*" It's not wrong to want attention or recognition; in fact those things are important. When the desire for these things becomes a consuming drive and God is pushed to the side so "I" takes over, it's pride. And pride is sin.

In order to sin, we must lie to ourself first. We must tell ourself, "The world centers around me and should serve me." Like Eve, we tell ourself, "I'll just take over God's position."

The sins of pride are deadly because they rob life. When we turn from pride we are turning from a passive attitude that has stopped us from doing anything about Satan's lies. When we face the cross and look up to Jesus Christ hanging there taking our place for the lies we have acted upon, we are in a place where there is no passivity. There is nothing passive about the cross. Because God has sacrificed Jesus for our sins and freed us from the chains of pride, we can aggressively take hold of the truth and live it.

You may want to re-read this chapter before going on. Pride has held you captive, defeated and sad; and God wants you free.

Dear Jesus,
I receive your loving touch now in my heart and mind. I want to understand and live in your loving-kindness, like David wrote of in the Psalms. I turn from pride as I now see it and recognize it in my life. Cleanse and renew me now, Lord. In Jesus' name. Amen.

CHAPTER FIVE

Why Can't I Be Satisfied?

Color Me Green

Picture one of your neighbors—the one who makes more money than you do; whose children get straight "A's" while yours come home with report cards they'd rather bury; whose spouse is more attractive than yours; whose lawn is always mown, raked and verdant green while yours is a briar patch with dandelion fur; whose car has two more cylinders than your car; who is younger and has a better job than you—isn't this fun?—who is healthier than you; who gets all the breaks you wish you had; who heralds from a wealthy family, the family you'd do anything to be a member of.

Now imagine driving along the freeway and

63

seeing the flashing light of a highway patrol car on the shoulder of the road. Someone has just been pulled over and the officer is writing a ticket. As you pass by and glance at the driver of the car, you realize it is your perfect neighbor!

What is your immediate feeling? Be honest now. Could it be that you feel the tiniest bit of delight?

Perhaps you would prefer to tell us you feel only sympathy for your poor neighbor. As for the rest of us mortals, however, when somebody who has more than we do receives something bad, we don't feel very sad about it. In fact, we usually feel quite delighted. Unfortunately that emotion is not very godly and indicates the presence of the deadly sin of envy. It can easily be diagnosed: If you feel miserable when you see the success of somebody else, you have it. (Or if you feel satisfaction from another's misfortune, you have it.)

Envy is not jealousy. Certain jealousy may be sinful, and yet other times it may be the appropriate desire to keep what is yours to yourself. It may be appropriate for a person to be jealous for his spouse. Notice we don't use the word "suspicious." "Jealous" and "suspicious" should not be used interchangeably. Godly jealousy in marriage refers to a desire to keep united that which God has sacredly united. There are times when jealousy is not appropriate—namely, when a thing is not rightfully ours. Jealousy, then, to be a godly emotion, must be motivated by the desire to guard what is rightfully ours. Envy is a different matter. Envy has nothing to do with what we already have. The envious person is worried about what *somebody else* has.

The envious person cannot tolerate somebody's having something he or she wants and cannot have.

Envy is a tormentor. Envy can make a person miserable from dawn till dusk, Sunday through Saturday. You will always find yourself exposed to people who have something you don't.

To be victorious, the Christian must come to grips with the fact that he is responsible for himself and he cannot control everything around him. An envious person, on the other hand, is never happy unless he can control things.

Try this exercise: On a piece of paper, list the things you think would make you happy. Maybe something like passing your final exams with straight "A's"; landing a higher-paying job; going on a clothes shopping spree; marrying the prince; feeling healthier; having acceptance from others; being respected, loved. You make your own list. Then review your list, noting items that indicate envy. You are probably more envious than you had expected. "A house like Shirley's," "to be as thin as Nancy . . ."

You cannot rid yourself of envy by sheer willpower. Envy is not an act, such as overeating or drunkenness or engaging in sexual sin. With willpower you can probably end such behaviors. But even if someone were to say to you, "If you will stop envying, I will give you a thousand-dollar bill," you couldn't do it. You need more than willpower to overcome envy.

Envy is the disposition to be unhappy because somebody else is happy. If someone is not a competitor of yours, or if he is not a threat to you, you may not envy him. For example, if one of your children receives a blessing in her life, you may not necessarily envy her. However, if the same child has a trait you wish you had, or if she threatens you with her success, you will probably become envious. Changing your beliefs is the only cure for envy.

You may not be bothered if some poor soul who is worse off than you has some good thing happen to him—he poses no threat to you. But when somebody you view as a rival, such as a peer, sibling, or even your best friend, does well, you may envy with a passion.

When the envious person receives a blessing, it somehow doesn't seem as good as it should be. It loses its luster, its appeal. For instance, you are full of envy because your friend got a new car, so you buy one, too. Why aren't you happy now? You feel discontented because when you look at your car and realize that it is yours, you decide it can't be very good. Your friend's car is good, not yours. You will be happy only if your friend's car breaks down and yours doesn't. "He's suffering and I'm not" then becomes a comfort.

The old aphorism "The grass is always greener on the other side of the fence" becomes, "My grass may be green here, but it would look a lot greener if the grass across the fence died and turned brown."

The deadly sin of envy knows only one way to be happy and that is in someone else's downfall. Have you every heard comments like, "My friend might think he's pretty big stuff now that he has a new car, but he'll find out that a car is not the answer to all his problems," or "So-and-so may be pretty but remember, beauty is only skin deep, and she's probably a total idiot under that glamorous exterior," or "So-and-so is so smart—I hate him," or "He may be a wonderful singer today, but what will he do when his voice leaves him tomorrow?" or "Big deal if so-and-so received the raise at work. He will never be able to hold on to such a demanding job anyhow," or "Did you hear about so-and-so? Can you believe how rich and famous he is, and now he's sitting in jail?" Gratification at someone else's downfall comes from envy.

Low self-esteem not only accompanies pride, as we saw in the last chapter, it generates envy. There is a high correlation between pride and envy in this respect. If you are envious, your self-esteem will go down as somebody else's goes up. If you see someone whom you consider a peer or a rival having more than you, you will not only feel bad that he has it, but you will feel less a person because of it. Your unspoken self-talk may be, "His success just shows what a loser I am."

Your self-esteem may drop when you see that your neighbor has more money than you, or when you see someone who has more fame or talent than you. Your self-esteem takes a beating because someone else is superior to you.

Envy therefore eagerly exposes the defects of the other person. "Far be it from me to say something about the teacher," the envious person will drone in a hushed tone, "but, let me tell you, I know," or "I don't want to put anybody down, but I think people should be aware that back in 1978, so-and-so was arrested and charged with. . . ."

Martin Luther, in his explanation of the eighth commandment, "Thou shalt not bear false witness against thy neighbor," says, "We should fear and love God that we may not deceitfully belie, betray, slander, or defame our neighbor. But defend him, speak well of him, and put the best construction on everything."

The envious person has one thing he always accomplishes when he encounters other people. He ranks them either above or below himself. His main question is, "Should I look up to this person or look down on him?" Such ranking or categorizing is constant.

Can Envy Make You Neurotic?

The seven deadly sins correlate specifically with certain psychological disorders. The sin of envy is often accompanied by depression. Depression indicates sorrow. If the score on the MMPI scale* in depression is high, envy will be high, too. John of Damascus, over 1200 years before the MMPI test was developed, said that envy and sloth are two things that are filled with sorrow. Envy is sorrow over another's good, and sloth is sorrow in spite of one's own spiritual good. Sloth, envy and depression go together like mud and a rainstorm, though one does not cause the other.

There is also a correlation between envy and introverson. A person who is shy, anxious, afraid to say anything that might upset someone, or afraid to make a mistake may be more envious than the person who is outgoing. Self-talk is the clue. The introverted person is saying, "I know that I am inferior in *comparison* with other people."

The introverted person maintains his reserved manner because he doesn't want anyone to discover his inferiority. He wants other people to think all is well in his life. The self-talk of the introverted person includes statements like, "If I talk, I might make a mistake. A mistake will reveal what an inferior per-

---

The Minneapolis Multiphasic Personality Inventory, a psychological test widely used by psychologists in diagnosing and treating patients.

son I really am. I had better keep quiet and avoid intimacy, just to be safe." This self-talk is based on the misbelief, "It would be the end of the world if somebody discovered how inept or ignorant (or whatever) I am."

Cicely is sitting alone on a couch at a party while everyone else is having fun. She observes the other people talking and laughing, but she can't think of a thing to say or laugh about. She tells herself, "How terrible that all these people are able to talk and laugh and have a great time while I feel miserably tense and isolated." The misbelief here is, "I must be inferior if other people are laughing and I am not."

Cicely needs to learn it would not be the end of the world if others made the discovery that she is not perfect.

Perfectionism Isn't Being Perfect

Perfectionism is a sin of which we all at some time have been guilty. Contrary to what you may think, it is not the sin of wanting to be perfect. Those who want to be perfect are rushing into the arms of God, eager to do His will. Rather, perfectionism is the sin of saying, "I *must* be perfect and I *must* have everybody else perfect, too. I can't stand imperfection. It makes me depressed."

Perfectionism is wrong only when it is an "ism." A person's envy produces his negative and ungodly drive for perfectionism. Feelings and behaviors come from what you tell yourself.

Reaping the Results of Envy

Envy, unlike any of the other deadly sins, promises but one thing: unhappiness. The other sins each promise something that appears to be good. We usually commit sin because we think we are going to get something beneficial by doing so. The deadly sin of pride tells us that we should be on top and that nothing else is good enough for us. The deadly sin of anger promises us the satisfaction of getting even with our enemies, which will make us feel good. The deadly sin of greed tells us having more money, friends, possessions, prestige, etc., will be good for us. The deadly sins of lust and gluttony promise temporary sensual pleasures we tell ourselves would be good for us and that we deserve to enjoy. The deadly sin of sloth tells us that it will be good for us to let other people worry about being responsible and effective in life.

But envy is different. It promises nothing but wretched misery from start to finish. It's an insidious sin which many people are unable to diagnose in themselves.

If there is no payoff for envy, why do we tolerate it? If we were to ask ourself why we practice envy in our life, could we give ten answers? Or even three? Let's diagnose our envy and stop lying to ourself about it.

Some pastors are envious of those with larger churches and more acclaim. A pastor doesn't like to admit he's envious, so he may say things like, "Oh, how wonderful that the church down the street is building a new sanctuary to seat a thousand (even though our little church is barely getting by with our small building)." This is something we might call the "Good-Loser Syndrome." How many times do we all bluff our way through painful envy with falsely hearty tones in our voices as we congratulate somebody for something *we* want? It's very difficult to keep the color green from showing as we flash our fake smiles.

The "Good-Loser Syndrome" tries to sound pleased in the face of someone else's triumph, while we're sick with envy. We can, according to Romans 12, be transformed by the renewing of our mind so that we may prove what is good and acceptable and the perfect will of God in our life. Our mind becomes new when we refuse to tell ourself the lies we've believed for so long.

Have you been telling yourself any of the following lies?

Envy Misbeliefs

- "Someone is better than I am, therefore I am in a terrible situation for me."
- "Somebody is better than I am and it would be terrible if somebody discovered that fact."
- "Things should be the way *I* want them to be."
- "I must categorize everyone as to whether or not they are better than I am."
- "I cannot be happy if other people have more than I have."
- "Someone else should not do better or have more talent than I."
- "Other people should not live better than I."

In order to eliminate such misbeliefs in your life, you must counteract them with the truth. Begin by examining what you tell yourself. Then start to convince yourself of the truth.

The Truth About Envy

- It is not wrong to feel as good about myself as I do about others.

- It is not wrong for me to enjoy myself as I am right now.
- It is not wrong to believe my life is as happy as others.
- It is not wrong to fully appreciate what I own without comparing it with what someone else owns.
- It is not wrong to tell myself the work I do is as important as the work others do.
- It is not wrong to be glad when someone has more than I.

It really does not make any difference at all if somebody is better off than you are. It does not make any difference if someone has things you want or is possibly more talented than you. There will always be someone with an ability, trait, character disposition, skill or knowledge that you do not have. You can enjoy your life in spite of that.

If you categorize people as superior or inferior to you, you are cherishing an illusion. You may see the next-door neighbor who makes more money than you and feel unhappy about it, but is he *better* than you because he is richer than you? Does richer mean better? Al Capone was rich. Or does fame mean better? Jack the Ripper was famous. Or does power mean better? Jezebel had power. Idi Amin had power.

Our value as people comes through God. He has made us; He has loved us; He has redeemed us. That is why we have value and why nobody is inferior. When you understand this, you can become a friend instead of an enemy to yourself.

Giving Cures Envy

You will gain freedom from envy when you contribute to the well-being of somebody else. The more envious you are of a person, the more you need to advance his well-being. Such positive action will battle your misbeliefs. Love, not willpower, is what is needed. God gives you all the love you need. You have all you need to give to others.

Your Father also gives you every good and perfect gift. He will shower you with the good and perfect gifts that you need. Envy will keep you from receiving His personal gifts to you.

God's perfect gifts for you are without fault. He knows your every need. The question is, do *you* know your needs? Just because your neighbor has something you like and admire does not mean you need it also.

You can turn from envy and tell Jesus, *"I now choose to respect myself and enjoy who I am and what I have. I now choose to become a friend to myself as well as to others. I am learning to give, to love, and I am all Yours. In Jesus' name. Amen."*

CHAPTER SIX

The Angry Heart

Never Angry?

Carrie: I never get angry.

Harry: Never?

Carrie: Absolutely never. I'm really in control of my emotions.

Harry: I'm glad to hear that because I just hit your car in the parking lot.

Carrie: You did *what*?

Harry: I hit your car in the—

Carrie: I heard you the first time! I'm not deaf! What kind of an idiot are you to go around hitting other people's parked cars? How bad is it? Don't answer that. Oh, this is terrible!

Harry: I'm sorry I've made you angry.

Carrie: Me? Angry? Don't be silly. Ha-ha. I'm *not* angry. I told you I *never* get angry! Can't you understand that? I am totally in control of my emotions!

Do you say you never get angry?

Very few people can say they have *never* felt angry. Hidden or open rage plays a role in forming our personality and behavior.

Carrie, although quite angry, vigorously denied her angry feelings. She refused to think of herself as a person who indulged in such a terrible sin. The lie she believed was: It is bad to get angry because people who get angry are out of control. If I get angry, I'll be out of control and that would mean I'm a terrible person.

We included a chapter on anger in *Telling Yourself the Truth*; here we want to expand on why we accept the misbeliefs of anger as truth and how the sin of anger can be eliminated.

Satan has managed to propagate the idea among Christians that if one is a truly good Christian and filled with the Holy Spirit, he will never be angry at anybody or anything. Maybe you think this way, and like Carrie go through life smiling stiffly no matter what happens. In spite of any grievances, you manage to mutter, "Praise the Lord." You tell yourself, "No matter what happens to me and no matter what anybody does to me, I'll *never* show anger."

Where does such thinking take root? More than likely your first understanding of anger was that it was very, very naughty. Your parents and teachers usually gave greater rewards to the child who held in his anger than the one who expressed it. The untruth they fostered was, "A good child never gets angry." The devil would like you to believe that, too, but remember, he is a liar. He specializes in deceiving people.

Jesus Was Angry

Imagine this scene: John, the friend of Jesus, is hurrying to keep pace with his new-found Master as He presses through the crowds of people in the inner court of the temple. It's hot and John is breathing heavily as he tries to maintain Jesus' strong stride. Sweat drips from his face and forehead. He then notices the expression on Jesus' face. John is surprised because Jesus' face is not reflecting His usual gentleness.

The Lord's jaw is tightened. His eyes dart from one money-changing vendor to another. The arteries in His temples throb and His dark brows produce a frown. He twists the leather cords in His hand around His wrist. Suddenly His stride turns into a near-run and He slaps the leather cords across the table of a vendor selling pigeons to worshipers. The vendor gasps with astonishment. Without a word, Jesus heaves a table on its side, and then another. The animals being sold bolt with alarm. The vendors scramble clumsily for their money rolling in all directions. John watches in awe as the Savior of the world pours out His godly anger upon those who made God's house a den of thieves. John may have thought of the words recorded in Deut. 32:21, "They have provoked me to anger with their vanities."

Do the Apostle Paul's words, "Be ye angry and sin not" (Eph. 4:26), contradict Jesus' behavior in this instance? Understand this: Jesus became furious but *He never sinned* in all His life. His anger was not sin. If Jesus was angry and did not sin, then it must be possible for us to experience anger without sin.

Anger as Emotion and Sin

Paul admonishes us to be angry, then qualifies the statement with, "sin not." These words make a distinction between the *emotion* of anger and the *sin* of anger.

The *emotion* of anger is designed by the Creator. He has given us the capacity to give an appropriate response to hurt and injury. The *sin* of anger, however, is self-centered and festers in the heart like an open sore.

Neither kind of anger is something you would want to maintain in your life. Even if you became angry in a godly way, with righteous indignation like the Lord Jesus experienced in the temple court, you would find yourself uncomfortable in that state. It never feels good to be angry.

Remember the last time you were angry and lashed out at someone? Such anger is inordinate. Inordinate anger is accompanied by the desire for revenge. The early church fathers defined inordinate as "beyond the bounds of what is reasonable or correct or godly." The *sin* of anger is an inordinate desire to take revenge, to fight back, rather than let God handle things. You would be showing inordinate anger if someone stole your watch or camera and, instead of forgiving them, you prayed earnestly for misfortune to strike them.

Psychological Disorders and Anger

The deadly sin of anger often accompanies the deadly sin of envy.

It also often accompanies a tendency toward obsessive compulsiveness. An obsessively compulsive person is perfectionistic; anxious; worrisome; never satisfied with himself, anyone or anything; and ever aware of everyone else's shortcomings. He becomes infuriated when things aren't right and people don't do as they "ought."

Anger is prevalent in paranoia (when a person is angry, suspicious and resentful of other people). A paranoid person may appear sensitive, but he is *self-*sensitive, not people-sensitive. Anger is also the predominant emotion in schizophrenia.

The introverted person who seems harmless and sweet may be full of anger and envy. He observes the happy lives of other people and angrily fumes, "Why can't *I* be happy?"

When a person experiences anger because other people are not paying attention to him or her, he or she may commit violent acts in order to be noticed. He may be enraged at his inability to do what other people are doing, so he wishes people would die or at least have as hard a time as he has.

Symptoms of Anger

People who know you well can tell when you are angry because they have learned to detect how your voice rises in pitch—even though you may say, "Who's angry? *I'm* not angry." They have learned to recognize the stiff jaw, the clenched teeth, the patronizing smile.

You know you are angry when you stop calling people by their nicknames or when you speak in syllables instead of sentences; when you withdraw and won't speak at all; when you hold back affection to loved ones and refuse to be giving and loving; when you lose sleep and develop headaches and stomach pains as you think of the injustices meted out to you.

Anger can contribute to psychosomatic disorders. Such physical problems as headaches, ulcers, hypertension, digestive and intestinal problems, and arthritis can be related to anger. These disorders may not always be caused by anger, but anger can be a major contributing factor.

Sometimes we may even treat anger itself as a physical disorder. Someone will say, "I have this temper"—as though it were a wart or a common cold. Their temper, which lashes out at people and hurts them, is hardly as innocuous as a wart. Sometimes we will indulgently put up with temper outbursts of our friends or loved ones using the excuse that they have the pathetic, hopeless disease of anger. They "just can't help themselves."

The deadly sin of anger tends to cling to a person like a noose around the neck. Whether just or unjust, inordinate or incomensurate, it seems to hang on forever. We stew, fret and even make ourself sick. Apart from God's truth and power, we cannot free ourself.

A Case of Anger

Janice is an attractive young woman whose husband left her and four children five years ago. When the marriage broke up, Janice's life was shattered and she thought she would never recover. She resigned from her job because she couldn't do her work properly while her mind was unable to concentrate. Her fears flowed easily and often she would sink into such despair that she could not carry on a conversation with co-workers.

While at home she spent her days eating, sleeping, watching TV, and eating some more. In three months' time she gained sixty pounds. Her despair deepened.

She talked to her friends about her husband and discovered he was seeing another woman. Janice's response was to cry and moan, and wonder what she had done wrong. She soon blamed herself for her husband's abandoning the family, and her guilt became so deep it manipulated nearly all her behaviors. She was no longer kind and outgoing, but sullen and bitter. Anger had taken its toll.

Janice often vented her anger at the children's expense. She yelled at them, scolded irrationally and was quick-tempered to the point of cruelty. However, neither her friends nor her family ever heard her express anger at what her husband had done to her.

Janice did not even consider the possibility that she could be filled with anger toward the man. She would sigh, smile tightly and say such things as, "I'm praying for my husband."

Before a person can do anything about his anger, he must admit that he feels anger. In order to remove something that is standing in one's way, one must first of all recognize that it's there. If a person admits he has anger somewhere within himself, he can start to get rid of it.

Janice thought she was being a good person by not admitting anger. Somewhere in her youth she had learned anger is bad. And she had learned it is especially bad for a woman to feel anger. So she unloaded her anger on her children and then blamed them for her outbursts. Her guilt grew to enormous proportions. She became like a walking keg of dynamite, hating and denying anger, yet spewing it like a geyser daily.

Janice didn't date other men. She became grossly overweight and reclusive. She believed if her husband had rejected her, all men would. In all this time Janice did not express her anger appropriately. When she came into therapy she complained of depression and lack of energy. She felt debilitated by life's demands on her. Though outraged by these demands and infuriated beyond control, she never once admitted her rage. Her discovery that she actually did feel anger was a cathartic experience. Her eyes flashed and her face became distorted as a sneer twisted her mouth. "I hate him," she said in agony. "I hate him. *I hate him!*"

After Janice had expressed her rage, she immediately felt guilty. It was so painful that she tried to deny her feeling of anger. She repeated her typical and familiar denial: "I pray for him, poor soul. I don't really hate him."

Janice had to learn that it was all right for her to feel angry, that only after she realized her rage could her healing come. She had been to many prayer meetings and received prayer for physical disorders (including her obesity) which were linked to her rage. Nothing had helped. She had seen doctors and even undergone surgery for a chronic stomach ailment, but her pains persisted. When she finally came for Christian therapy, she was considering more surgery, though she did not actually need it. When Janice was able to say, "I have anger," she could take the next step in overcoming it.

Anger is not as horrible as the denial of it. Even good Christians get angry. Often the reason people do not express their anger is because others tell them this would be unacceptable. If someone you love were to say, "I feel angry right now and here's why," could you quietly listen as he explained his feelings to you? Could you resist offering advice or argument when he is finished? Could you smile, take his hands and say, "Thank you for telling me"? Most people feel obligated to give advice, or argue when another person has said something important, rather than affirm the legitimacy of the person's anger.

Janice had never before expressed her angry feelings, not because there was no one to whom she could talk, but because she had not allowed herself to admit she felt anger. The treacherous aspect of Janice's anger is that if she did not admit to herself and express constructively in *words* that she felt anger, she would express it in actions. She would shout, hit, criticize, hurt herself and others, as well as become physically ill—all destructive behaviors.

Making Anger Constructive

It is not true that a good Christian never gets angry. If your father or mother frequently screamed and yelled with rage, rather than controlling their anger, you may still perceive anger as terrible and destructive. It was so frightening to you when you were young that you came to believe your own anger is equally destructive. It was painful for you to witness other people fighting with each other. Perhaps you have seen violence and rage in action and you learned that anger is terrible. You now may have within yourself a mixture of guilt and fear about anger.

When you hold your anger in and finally explode with fury, you are committing the very sin you are trying to hide from yourself. If you will admit your anger to the Lord *before* the tantrum, you will open the doors to truth and remove the power of the lie that anger is always evil and frightening.

Sometimes it seems safer to the angry person to remain quiet about the anger in order not to compound the problem. We have often asked patients, "Have you told your spouse about your anger?" The response has typically been, "Oh, no. It would be pointless to do that. It would only start an argument." The answer is not true, masked by deceit. The truth probably is, "It would be too painful to express my true feeling because my spouse might retaliate in such a way as to prove what a nothing I really am."

The lie must be counteracted with truth. We all are vitally important people. It is a lie that we are worthless, no matter what we have experienced in life. Even if our parents abandoned us, if we flunked a grade in school, if we spent time in prison, if we failed at marriage or at child-rearing, it makes not one dot of difference. We are precious and important to God. God sent His Son Jesus to the cross to die for us.

We believe if you were the only person on this earth, God would have sent Jesus for your sake alone. If you have given your life to God and accepted Jesus as your Savior, to save you from your sins and misbeliefs, rest assured that you belong to Him. The first thing to do with the misbelief "I am worthless" is to replace it with the truth. You are not worthless. In God's sight you are priceless.

How to Conquer Anger

Once we have brought our anger into the open, with the Holy Spirit's help, we can begin to make the needed changes. We need the work of the Holy Spirit within us to lead us into all truth. Jesus called Him the "Spirit of Truth." He shows us that the misbegotten, misdirected sin of anger is based on lies. In order to commit this sin, we must tell ourselves certain untruths such as it is all right to practice inordinate anger and remain angry. Jesus tells us not to let the sun set on our anger because He has given us the daily power to deal with our problems.

Let us examine the lies associated with anger so that we can recognize them immediately when they occur in our mind.

Misbelief: *"Somebody or something else made me mad. My anger has nothing to do with personal responsibility. I'm mad and it's all their fault."* The belief that one's emotional state is caused by the environment is most prevalent in anger. It is related to a major untruth which says, "I am not worth much." Whenever somebody does something that we think we have the right to be angry about, we should search our misbeliefs. Maybe we are construing the other person as signaling a message that we are not important. If we are not important, that means we are no good. If we are not important and are no good, then we do have something to be upset about.

Consider the times your feelings have been hurt. You probably were telling yourself that it was terrible your value was not being appreciated. Somebody hadn't recognized your achievements or your positive attributes. Maybe they didn't say hello to you when they were supposed to, or didn't invite you to their party, or maybe they ignored you when you wanted their attention.

Next time you're offended and you become very angry, immediately ask yourself, "What am I telling myself? Am I telling myself that person must think I am not worth much and therefore I have the right to be angry?"

The last time you were upset and everybody around you was wondering what was wrong, did you even for a moment consider your attitude and behavior sinful? You can behave in the most ugly, unloving manner and never realize it because you are firmly convinced you have every right to be upset.

Misbelief: *"I have every right to get all upset when things go wrong."* Why argue for the right to give yourself an ulcer? To drive up your blood pressure? Getting upset is *not* one of your basic inalienable rights.

Tell yourself you have the right to joy unspeakable instead of anger and misery. Your "rights" include abundant life, peace, wisdom and joy. It is not the end of the world if you're not accepted by one and all.

Misbelief: *"I can't cope when people don't accept me."* It's nice to be accepted, but not always possible. It may be disagreeable and unpleasant not to be accepted, or unjustly criticized, but you will eventually recover. You may not like it, but you can still go on living very happily.

Misbelief: *"Everyone should treat me the way I want them to."* God has made it clear from the time you were a little tot in Sunday school, that you are going to live in a world where there are sinners—a lot of them. Even Christians may not always behave in an acceptable and approvable manner.

You will have rewarding relationships in your life once you exercise a new attitude toward people. When you allow others the right to make mistakes, you will be easier to live with. When you drop your urge to control people and situations, you will find yourself more relaxed in your relationships. Others will sense your ease and acceptance and be drawn to you. Love and forgiveness are irresistible. You will tend to treat people well when you admire them, and they will reciprocate.

If you expect to be treated well, and your unspoken demands go unmet, you will become angry. Angry people are rarely respected or admired.

Misbelief: *"I have a bad temper and I can't help it. I just can't control anger."* When you start telling yourself the truth—"I *can* control my behavior"— you will find that you can be free of the bad habits you thought were in your very blood.

By telling yourself you can't control your anger, you open yourself to such lies as, "I can't control my eating (or drinking, or smoking, or whatever other bad habits I have)." Unfortunately, your friends may respond to your destructive behavior by accepting it. Then you're even worse off. "Go ahead, Bill, you poor fellow," they infer, "you've got this genetic weakness with your temper and you just can't help it. That's all right, old boy, go right ahead and destroy yourself and everyone around you. You just can't help yourself."

Sound ridiculous? Sad to say, millions of people are doing that very thing right now. Their friends stand by watching them go further and further into the quicksand of defeat and do nothing but smile dismally and wave as they sink. "Poor old Max. Did you hear he had a heart attack? Poor guy. I'll bet it was because of that rotten temper he always had." Anger can contribute to a multitude of physical problems. It can even be a contributing cause of premature death.

You cannot control and conquer anger by expressing rage, by screaming and hitting things, in order to show the world how you feel.

Destructive expression of anger by yelling, hitting or hurting someone is not acceptable in any circumstance. It is not a laughing matter when a child kicks his feet, juts out his little lower lip and acts out his temper (his misbelief being twofold, "I have the right to have a temper tantrum when things don't go the way I want them to," and "I should always get what I want"). Mommy may giggle, "Oh, isn't little Billy adorable when he gets angry?" But this temper is not funny. Whether a person is five or ninety-five, if he screams in rage at those around him, he is under the false assumption that he is exclusive, that he does not have to learn to care about other people, or tell himself the truth even if he doesn't feel like it.

An adult slamming his fist against the wall is no different than the little child lying on the floor screaming and kicking his feet when he doesn't get what he wants. "Letting it all hang out" is not the answer. A person *can* control his temper—by controlling his misbeliefs.

You must bring your anger under control. Life or God or others owe you nothing. Neither does anyone *make* you angry. You make yourself angry.

Anger is sin when it is uncontrolled, destructively or maliciously vented or expressed. Denial and repression of anger aid sin because they are based on lies.

Anger is a simple emotion when it is expressed in conversation and when it is not allowed to go unattended. "Let not the sun go down upon your wrath" means you *can* be in charge of your feelings. You *can* live a fulfilling life with your emotions under your control.

CHAPTER SEVEN

When More Is Never Enough

The deadly sin of greed has one lie upon which hinge all others. That lie is, "Having 'X' would be good for me and I *must* have it." Greed tells me that whatever my eye takes a fancy to should belong to me because it would be good to have it. I believe I can never be happy unless I have 'X'.

Each of the seven deadly sins requires the lie that sin holds some benefit for us. However, sin holds no benefits, only curses. Ahab's greedy lusting after Naboth's vineyard is a good example (see Chapter One). His greed caused him to murder. Once he had the vineyard, he was still unhappy, and he and his family were destroyed. No matter what we gain out of greedy motives, we will never know true peace and joy in our achievements. Peace and joy come directly from the heart of God through the Spirit of God. They are the fruit of the pure and holy heart. When we plant holy seeds, we get holy fruit. Greed has no place here.

How to Recognize Greed

You are greedy if:

- You become undone and miserable after losing even the smallest amount of money.
- You become very disturbed when after having bought an item you discover you could have purchased it cheaper somewhere else.
- You receive an inordinate amount of pleasure handling and counting money.
- When the store forgets to bill you for an amount you owe, you do nothing about it.
- You make plans for securing a job that pays a lot of money rather than a job you find interesting and rewarding.
- You feel that paying income tax is robbery and so you cheat at tax time.
- You feel sick when somebody else buys something you want but can't afford.
- You feel uneasy around people who are better off than you and tell yourself it's because they're "snobs" and you are "just plain folk."
- When the conversation turns to what someone has recently purchased, you always tell of *your* recent purchases.
- You have a catalogue (your "wish book") and you drool with longing every time you look at its expensive and luxurious items.
- You often drive through neighborhoods better

than yours and yearn to live in one of those exclusive homes.

- When you give something away, you want to be sure your generosity will be reciprocated.
- When you go to a buffet-style restaurant, you feel obliged to eat until you can hardly stand up because the sign says, "All You Can Eat," and you want your money's worth.

A recent article in *Time* magazine says Americans are buying $1,300 worth of merchandise on credit for every $1,000 they earn. How do we explain this kind of behavior? Are we naïve? Anyone who knows arithmetic is aware that if we spend $1,300 when we've only got $1,000, we're headed for trouble. Do we excuse this behavior by saying we're obsessive compulsives and don't know what we're doing? Shall we tell ourselves we just can't help ourselves? Of course not. The problem is *greed*.

Possessions for Possessions' Sake

Examples of greed and covetousness are simple enough to see. Owning things for their own sake is coveting. The greedy person just plain wants to have it *all*. The greedy person craves possessions and more possessions just for possessions' sake.

Have you ever had a collection of anything? Don't worry, collecting things does not mean you are riddled with the sin of greed. Many people are collectors. Maybe you save string or paper bags for future use; that is probably not greed. Collecting becomes greed only if you save things you will never use because you just can't bear to throw them away.

How about a hobby—collecting things that are

important to you such as stamps, art, antique books, or anything you really like. Such collections will reflect greed only if you find yourself enslaved to them by hoarding and anxiously competing with somebody else's collection.

In Moliere's play *The Miser*, the main character is Harpigon, whose name is derived from the Greek word *harpe* meaning "claw." He is a caricature of the greedy person whose claws rip at the world, tearing and clamoring to get things for himself. This is actually idolatry. The Bible teaches us to keep ourselves from idols. If we view what we own and find that we have made a god out of our stamp collection or fine china or flower garden or stock portfolio, we must repent of idolatry.

First Tim. 6:10 says, "For the love of money is the root of all evil: which while some coveted after, they have erred from the faith, and pierced themselves through with many sorrows." All of the seven deadly sins are roots of evil. It is in this sense that evil causes suffering, hurt and pain. If you are caught up in one or all of these sins, you and others will suffer. Sin comes with destruction as standard equipment. God does not stand on a distant cloud with a big club waiting to get us every time we feel greedy. He is a God of love who gently guides us into truth so that we can live happily, free of the sorrow and agonies which sin brings. We punish *ourselves* with sorrow when we sin.

If greed is one of your problems, you can teach yourself new behaviors which will lead to joy and freedom from sin. This happened to Charles Dickens' Scrooge. Scrooge exemplified the deadly sin of greed, and he was certainly an unhappy man. He was rich enough to have anything a man could want, including a successful business and a loving family, but he was utterly miserable and lonely.

Do not confuse the sin of greed with the sin of envy; they are very different. If I envy you for what you have, I want what you have only because it's yours and not mine. As soon as I have it, I am not very interested in it. The items I want are fascinatingly and obsessively important to me only if you own them. My own possessions are not very valuable to me simply because they are mine. What *you* own is valuable to me because it seems more important.

Greed is like a claw. It digs in its nails and pulls toward oneself and possesses. Greed or covetousness is the excessive love of possessing things with the intent to have them and hold them to oneself. The key word in greed, as in anger, is *inordinate*, or out of order.

God knows what is good for us, what is "in order." He knows how to keep us from suffering and want. He does not provide for each of us exactly the same. Sometimes we will experience hard times in order to learn not to set our hearts on the treasures of earth. If we are trusting God we can see that greed is as debilitating as a disease. Jesus tells us, "Take no thought for the morrow." Greed is not only taking thought for tomorrow, but hoarding for tomorrow. The greedy person will begin to worry about the next meal even before he has finished the one he is eating.

The Holy Squeeze

God always prospers His children. If we set our heart on *God*, we will prosper. If we set our heart on prospering, we may become greedy and envious.

A minister friend of ours was once in a financial

squeeze because his income was irregular. He could hardly make ends meet from one check to another. He told the Lord, "I can't understand why this is happening to me. If you would prosper me, I wouldn't have to spend so much time praying about paying these bills. Just think of all the time I could spend helping people and serving you better." He now tells of the great lesson he learned when the Lord answered him and said, "Now, my son, you are really learning how to *pray!*"

If you find yourself in a "squeeze," bless it. It could be your *holy squeeze.* Gain all you can from it. Many times when a Christian is in financial trouble, instead of using the experience for the glory of God and learning the lessons of prayer, he or she will slip into greed and envy. Our minister friend could have resorted to such feelings. He could have observed other ministers with large, financially successful ministries and felt jealous. He could have coveted their success. But covetousness would have contaminated his ministry. The seventh commandment, "Thou shalt not covet. . . ," means we can not ache for anything our neighbor has, including his spouse, servants, livestock or possessions. This commandment tells us to stop wishing longingly that we could have a coat like Mrs. Smith's coat, and it also tells you to stop groaning about Joe's thick, curly hair if yours is thin and wispy. If we tell ourselves we've just got to have what they've got, we're coveting and in for much unhappiness and discontent.

Is Desire Wrong?

We must discern greed from desire. Desire is a gift from God. Life without desire is a dull and futile life; psychologists say that without desire a person will not even get out of bed in the morning. Without desire, life stops.

The commandments against greed and covetousness are not against the natural desires within us which have been created by God himself. The commandments speak against warped desires, not godly desires and motives.

It is perfectly legitimate to desire a nice home, a new dining room table, shrubs along the driveway, new clothes, a better job, or a car that run's smoothly. There is no inherent sin in desiring these things. Even to desire something that belongs to another person does not mean we are covetous and hopelessly lost in greed. If we are walking through a parking lot and see a new car and think, *Oh, I'd love to have a car like that*, we have not sinned. The desire becomes sin when we tell ourselves, "I've *got* to have that car." Sin occurs when our thoughts center solely around that car; when we begin to plan how we are going to get that car no matter what; when we fantasize about how essential it is to possess that car.

Greed refuses to be denied the thing it wants to possess. Desire, on the other hand, is not troubled by the lack of that thing.

Greed and Irritability

When you receive a letter in the mail from a Christian ministry asking for money, do you get irritated? When you open a letter that begins, "Dear Christian Friend, we need your help...," do you grumble, "Don't they know I'm not made of money?"

When your pastor preaches on stewardship and tithing, do you sigh, "Oh, no. Here it comes. They're going to take another offering"?

Do you argue with your siblings about who pays the most to care for your aging parents?

Do you feel imposed upon every time one of your children asks for money to buy something?

Do you resent the purchases your wife wants to make and insist upon controlling the finances yourself, even to the point of buying her clothes for her?

Would losing a $20 bill ruin your day?

The deadly sin of greed is often excused by others because sometimes it sounds acceptable. If a person brags at a party about the profits acquired on his stock certificates and investments, he is considered smart, not greedy. Because greed can appear as "smart," "thrifty," "economical" or "clever," a person can be suffering from its sorrows without even knowing why he is so unhappy and dissatisfied.

Donna is a young woman who believed all of her problems were caused by other people. She was distressed at the insurance company which refused to pay her workman's compensation for injuries she insisted she sustained on her job. She could reel off a long list of physical problems and complaints that she alleged resulted from working conditions at the company where she was employed. The physicians she saw, and they were many, all agreed that her problems were "in her mind." They told her she had a nervous condition and prescribed tranquilizers.

At her church Donna went foward for healing every time she had a chance, but she received very little relief each time she had prayer for healing. Why? Because she tenaciously clung to misbeliefs regarding her physical condition, and they all sprang from greed.

"I need money and the insurance company should

give it to me," she would moan. "Don't they know I hurt?" This statement shows she misbelieved it is good to hurt in order to receive money. Telling herself that her pains were caused by her work, she continued to lie and deceive herself, avoiding the truth that pain was not a good thing to have.

Donna also believed that she was not distorting the truth. She believed she had a right to feel bad, no matter what. After all, that money would be good for her. She was convinced that other people had caused all her problems and those people would have to change if she was ever to be happy. Those people who refused her workman's compensation were at fault. It was an outrage.

Do you see the sin of Ahab here as Donna insisted she must get what she wanted *or else*? Do you see that Donna's sin of greed was her acceptance of lies?

Conquering Greed

The fundamental untruth behind greed is, "Having _____ would be good for me and I ought to have it. I cannot stand not having _____. If I don't have it, I can never be happy. If I lose it, my life will be ruined. I must have what I want."

You can stop considering it a tragedy that you do not have what somebody else has. You are only kidding yourself when you tell yourself possessions will make you feel better or that owning something someone else has will make you more important. God says you already *are* important.

Jesus came to set you free from the many sorrows of sin. The sin of greed can bring much sorrow. When you find yourself tempted to covet what somebody else has, or to feel depressed at the happy news of someone else's blessings, tell yourself immediately, "I do not need to have what someone else has. I can survive without the possessions, recognition, achievement, and talents of other people. I can be happy without them. I do not have to have, be, or do what somebody else has, is or does. I can be perfectly happy with less than others. I can be completely content with *me*."

CHAPTER EIGHT

Laziness, the Blues and Depression

Mike complains of constant nervousness, guilt and fear. He has the inescapable feeling that something dreadful is about to happen. Afraid he will not be able to handle his job, he has a strong impulse to resign. Whatever he is doing, he worries that he should be doing something else. He constantly afflicts himself with negative self-talk. He castigates himself for lacking enough trust in God; he tells himself he is lazy and self-indulgent for avoiding the things he does not like.

Mike has a strong desire to learn but is afraid that education is worldly. He complains of "butterflies" in his stomach, and has difficulty concentrating when he tries to read or study. Mike expects to be rejected by his peers, to be fired from his job eventually. He finds it difficult to make decisions and when forced to make a decision, he is tense and unhappy. Because he overeats, he is overweight. He also believes women don't really care for him, so he is afraid if he becomes romantically involved with a woman she will only hurt him. He is plagued with the fear he may be homosexual.

Mike's deadly sin is *sloth*. What he tells himself robs him of joy in nearly every life situation. His self-talk reveals considerable guilt and depression. He talks constantly of shoulds, oughts and musts. His expectations are distorted so he is riddled with guilt.

A slothful person typically believes a number of false notions. First, he is a type of performer, acting out life on a stage. He believes that his performance is the most crucial matter in all the world. He tells himself that the performance at hand is so crucial and vital that God is glaring with an ever-punitive eye to make sure it's done right. The slothful person believes God expects an exacting performance and demands perfection in every way; He then sits back and smugly watches him or her fail.

The slothful person, like Mike, creates goals that are always more rigid and demanding than he or anybody else could possibly fulfill. Sloth, you may be surprised to know, is related to pride. The slothful person believes that only superior people have the highest standards, and that superior people have higher goals and loftier ideals than mere ordinary people. This mixture of pride and sloth induces enormous stress because the slothful person knows that he or she cannot live up to such towering goals and demands. The result is condemnation and guilt.

Mike is a Christian but isn't sure there are any real privileges to be had by being one (other than going to heaven when he dies). He has developed the misbelief that life is not worth living because he really does not know if he can trust God to answer his prayers or to arrange circumstances to reward him now. He despairs of the future and sees no hope in it. He doesn't see how he can ever get any better. Mike believes his choices are so crucial that if he doesn't make the right choices, he may never recover. Naturally, with such dread of making wrong choices, he chooses to make no choices at all. Mike unconsciously views God as a hateful God, rather than a compassionate God who loves him.

A Definition of Sloth

In Heb. 6:12 we are told, "Be not slothful, but followers of them who through faith and patience inherit the promises." This must mean there can be sloth among believers. If we were to take a poll of every person on earth and ask, "Have you ever been depressed?" the responses would indicate that nearly everyone has been depressed at some time in life.

In the counseling office we hear conversations like this: "I've felt very down for two months and I don't know what's the matter with me. I've tried to get a hold of myself, but the harder I try, the worse I feel. I no longer want to do anything. I'm letting my whole life fall apart; my apartment looks just terrible and I've lost contact with my friends."

A general feeling of depression and guilt indicates the presence of sloth. "I just don't feel like I can talk to God anymore. I'm afraid to go to church and Christian fellowship. The last time I went to Bible study, I told them how I felt and they just told me I was full of self-pity. They said all I needed to do was stop feeling sorry for myself and I would be all right. I tried, but I didn't improve. Now I'm afraid to go back to Bible study because they'll be mad at me for not getting better."

Such a scene could be duplicated many times in the counselor's office. It is especially typical because Christians usually scold each other for being depressed. If you are depressed now, or dealing with people who are depressed, we hope this chapter will help you understand that the remedy is not brickbatting the depressed person to his senses by simply advising him to stop feeling sorry for himself.

I am practicing self-pity if I coddle or pamper myself with the underlying belief that I deserve much better than the rotten deal I am getting in life. If I am depressed, I do not pamper myself. I punish myself. I see little reason for anything good and am not motivated to do something rewarding for myself as self-pity would seek to do. Instead, I will seek to punish, hurt or remove something from myself.

Sloth is a habitual unwillingness to take positive action or to exert energy, be it physical, mental or spiritual.There are two signal emotions which indicate sloth is present. One signal is sorrow—sadness, the "blues." The other is carelessness—feeling so bad that the person no longer cares. Laziness and indolence become common.

John of Damascus called sloth "sorrow in the face of one's own spiritual good." Sorrow and carelessness are the two symptoms that show a need for the application of truth.

"The blahs" is how one person may describe the feelings of sloth. "I've got the blahs today" not only expresses sadness and carelessness, but a sense of heaviness. The depressed person often feels that a thousand-pound weight is strapped to each of his limbs. He bows his head down as though his back were carrying a great burden. He can hardly get out of bed in the morning; when the alarm clock buzzes the whole day looks like a mountain too difficult to climb. At such a time decisions and concentration are almost impossible. Reading Scripture seems like reading the telephone book. Praying seems like talking to the wall. When this happens it's time to counteract with your trusty weapon, truth.

Attacking the Blahs

Being depressed doesn't mean the rest of the world, including God, is depressed. I may feel so sad I can't hold a consistent conversation with the Lord, but that doesn't mean He won't speak to me. My defeated feelings don't defeat Him. He still loves, guides, protects and encourages me. Such negative feelings are built on lies—lies of the enemy telling me how rotten things are, what a loser I've always been and how terrible the future looks. He may even try to convince me that I am ill, that there is something wrong with my mind.

Although depression is linked with the chemistry of the brain, usually depression is caused by misbeliefs, not chemistry. Most depressed persons have no underlying illness that causes the psychological disorder; they *talk* themselves into depression.

Depression is not a benign problem at which I can snap my fingers and make it go away. But *depression is not hopeless.* If I am depressed now, the chances that I will stay depressed are very, very low. Almost zero. The good news is, I *can* overcome depression. I can recover from depression even without treatment if I begin to combat the lies I have been believing.

It won't do any good just to tell myself to stop feeling sorry for myself. The cause of depression is not self-pity, despite popular beliefs to the contrary. Very seldom have we seen a person whose depression is caused by self-pity. Depression is a direct result of believing lies such as "I'm a loser" or "I'm not as good as someone else." It is *not* true that I am a loser just because my boyfriend broke up with me, for example, or because I lost my job or got an "F" on my French exam.

The truth is, I am loved by God and that puts me in a position to cope with loss. Even if I have failed, I can recognize that fact that I am still important.

We tend to judge our worth by our performance, leaving no room for error (at least not big mistakes). We easily believe the accusations that we are worthless because the demands we put on ourselves are unreasonable. To be depressed because someone else has "done me wrong" is to believe essentially the same lies; we are giving someone else power to render us helpless. We are saying, "I have no solutions to this dilemma. I was fired unjustly so I submit to behaving as a defeated, worthless person."

The first lie we believe is, *"I'm no good,"* with the accompanying thoughts and self-talk being, "I'm a failure" and "I can't do anything right."

The second lie is, *"My life is unbearable."* The accompanying thoughts and self-talk are, "I can't tolerate any more; this is more than I can bear."

The third lie is, *"There's no hope for me."* This is cluttered with such thoughts and self-talk as, "My life will never get better; there's no hope for my future."

The root lie is, "It is *good* for me to be defeated."

By believing these lies, we are agreeing with the devil that it is better to listen to Satan than to listen to God. Our interpretation of worth therefore needs to be challenged and changed.

Mike, the man we mentioned at the beginning of the chapter, considered himself worthless. Here is a sample of our conversation.

Mike: I'm a failure. I am such a dud.

Therapist: Oh? Why do you say that?

Mike: I don't know, I just am. I'm a failure.

Therapist: Did you ever do anything in your life that was not a failure?

Mike: Not really. I've always been a failure.

Therapist: Did you finish high school?

Mike: . . . Yes.

Therapist: What kind of grades did you get?

Mike: I had a "B" average in high school, but I didn't really study very hard or try.

Therapist: Is a "B" average a failure?

Mike: No, I guess it isn't a failure, but I could have done better.

Therapist: That isn't what you're calling yourself. You're not calling yourself a person who could do better; you're calling yourself a failure.

Mike: Well, I don't know.

Therapist: Did you ever have a job?

Mike: Yes.

Therapist: How did you perform on your job?

Mike: I did all right, I suppose. The people there were not fair though.

Therapist: Did you fail?

Mike: No, I quit.

Sloth prefers to quit to keep from failing. In this way, as Mike did, he can call himself a failure even though he never really gave himself a chance to fail.

Mike said he could not get up in the morning, that his life was not worth living. But one day his brother dragged him out of bed and insisted he play tennis with him. Mike argued, "I don't like to play tennis." (Naturally, he didn't. He was afraid he would fail at it.) Undeterred, his brother took him to the court, gave him a racket, served him the ball. Lo and behold, Mike lobbed it back. After the game, which he played very well, he told his brother, "That really wasn't so bad after all!"

If Mike had quickly resumed his self-maligning self-talk, his momentary relief from pain would have disappeared. He would have quickly resumed being depressed if he had refused to admit he enjoyed the round of tennis. His tennis skill showed clearly that he was not a failure. Even if he had played a poor game, he was not a failure. The point is, he could play.

The misbelief "I have no hope" is impossible according to the Word of God. Jesus has risen from the dead, triumphed over death and the devil. Because of His resurrection from the dead, we can be resurrected from the ways of sin. We can change. We can experience new vitality and power in our lives where there once was sin and despair. Christ is *in* us and we now are miraculously able to appropriate and live in the truth, "the mystery which hath been hid from ages and from generations, but now is made manifest to his saints: to whom God would make known what is the riches of the glory of this mystery among the Gentiles; which is *Christ in you*, the hope of glory" (Col. 1:26, 27).

What God Loves

If God sees a person sitting like a lump of pudding, upset, trembling, fearful and guilty, He does not swoon with delight and exclaim to all the angels, "Now, there's someone who really knows how to suffer!" Neither does He unsheath His long stick when the victim isn't matching up to his own expectations and give him a whack on the head yelling, "Shame!"

God loves us so much that instead of punishing us for every wrong thing we have done, He sent Jesus, not only to show us the way to be saved from the penalty of our sins, but to *identify* with us. He actually *became* our slothful depression. He knows every one of our misbeliefs and He knows what they sound like. He suffered because of them. God therefore identifies with our pain. He can say, "I know how you feel."

Heb. 2:17, 18 says, "He had to be made like his brethren in every respect, so that he might become a merciful and faithful high priest in the service of God, to make expiation for the sins of the people. For because he himself has suffered and been tempted, he is able to help those who are tempted" (RSV).

He is involved with our feelings. After all, He was "despised and rejected of men; a man of *sorrows* and acquainted with *grief*. . ." (Isa. 53:3). He knows what it's like to be put down: "I gave my back to the smiters, and my cheeks to them that plucked off the hair: I hid not my face from shame and spitting" (Isa. 50:6).

Scripture assures us "sin shall not have dominion over you" (Rom. 6:14). Jesus conquered sin by allowing it to overcome Him as He hung on the cross. He drank the cup of death in order that we could drink the cup of life. In the cross He destroyed the power of Satan. And now you can be alive, healed, forgiven and renewed because Jesus paid the price for forgiveness and victory.

Discovering Joy

The Bible tells us to put on the garment of praise for the spirit of heaviness. We have good reason to be joyful: Jesus' song of victory is, "I am the first and the last: I am he that liveth, and I was dead; and behold, I am alive for evermore, Amen; and have the keys of hell and death" (Rev. 1:18); Paul's declaration is, "Even when we were dead in sins, [God] hath quickened us together with Christ" (Eph. 2:5). Joy is the Christian's inheritance.

Some Christians live as though they are condemned forever. The Word of God doesn't tell us that. No! It is the nonbeliever who inherits the rewards of sin, without protection or the help of God. "There is no peace, sayeth the Lord, unto the wicked" (Isa. 48:22). The children of the Lord inherit the benefits of the Lord! Therefore, if we are experiencing the negative feelings and destructive thoughts of the nonbeliever, it's time to challenge and change. We are behaving like a person wearing somebody else's coat that doesn't fit. It's time to put on your own coat, "the new man, which after God is created in righteousness and true holiness" (Eph. 4:24).

"[God] hath made him to be sin for us, who knew no sin; that we might be made the righteousness of God in him" (2 Cor. 5:21). The moment we accept Jesus Christ as our Savior and confess Him as our Lord, and believe that God raised Him from the dead, He becomes our righteousness. The same power of God that made Jesus righteous has been given to us through our new birth in Him, for "as he is, so are we in this world." He is not defeated by sin.

What we are teaching here is not mental gymnastics, but a life empowered by the Holy Spirit of truth. We can become master of our circumstances. We can be confident in the work Jesus has done on the cross for us and live in victory over sin. We can *experience* the words, *"Nevertheless I live; yet not I, but Christ liveth in me"* (Gal. 2:20).

You may be engulfed in the sin of sloth and depressed feelings. Your strength to resist the devil's lies is undeveloped and weak. It's time now to acknowledge your weaknesses and realize that you *"can do all things through Christ"* who supernaturally strengthens you.

You can live victoriously. You can conquer the lies of Satan that have kept you depressed and blue. You are *not* a lazy person. You are a do-er because God is a do-er. You're a do-er of the Word! Rejoice in your deliverance from deception; rejoice in your escape from condemnation to acceptance, from captivity to freedom, from sorrow to joy and hopelessness to power.

Speak the truth to yourself and you will know you have accepted the beautiful fact that Christ lives in you and that you are constantly new and alive in Him:

"I am not lazy, not worthless, not joyless. I am filled with the Holy Spirit of God. I am free to be me and enjoy myself and my life. Jesus is my Lord and my identity."

CHAPTER NINE

Romance and Sexuality

Sam is seventeen. He has recently graduated from high school and is preparing for college. He comes to the therapist complaining of horrible thoughts he cannot stop, including killing cats and doing violent acts to people. He is deeply troubled about these uncontrollable thoughts because he is a vegetarian and believes that to kill animals is a sin. Sam has a number of compulsive rituals he goes through every night, including checking to make sure the lights are off, the doors are locked and the stove is off. More than anything, Sam worries about committing the "unpardonable sin." At times he does not know whether he has committed it or not, but at other times he is positive that he has. His guilt is overwhelming.

Gross sexual thoughts trouble Sam. Prevalent in

111

Sam's emotions are tension, conflict, anxiety and distress. Guilt over his sexual feelings and his anger cause him great unhappiness.

His parents view him in opposite ways. His mother is overly attentive to Sam's every need, always sympathetic and responsive to his emotions. She kisses and hugs him and hovers over him, "just to see that you're all right, honey." On the other hand, his father is distant and opposed to anything his mother does for him.

Sam greatly resents his father, although he would like a better relationship with him.

Sam is obsessed because he believes performing his rituals will prevent the unleashing of God's wrath upon him.

He believes he deserves to die in a horrible way because of his lustful feelings toward his mother and his angry, murderous, aggressive feelings toward his father.

Sam believes that his father stands in the way of his relationship with his mother and therefore ought to be eliminated. The lie he tells himself is, "It would be good for me if my father were dead and my mother were all mine." Resultantly, another untruth is, "I'm a terrible person for lusting after my mother and desiring to see my father dead. I deserve to die because God certainly is angry with me. I've committed the unpardonable sin."

Until Sam challenges the lies he believes, he will be unable to accept God's forgiveness. The first thing he must do is stop monopolizing his mother, releasing his emotional grip on her. As a second step he must stand on his own two feet (not mother's) to improve his relationship with his father. His misbeliefs are those of lust and anger. The problem is sin, not his guilty conscience—it has only surfaced to accuse him. His conscience has not helped him change his behavior.

In Matt. 5:27 we read, "Thou shalt not commit adultery: but I say unto you, That whosoever looketh on a woman to lust after her, hath committed adultery with her already in his heart." Jesus is so concerned about sin that He even said, "If your hand or your foot causes you to sin, cut it off and throw it away; it is better for you to enter life maimed or lame than with two hands or two feet to be thrown into the eternal fire. And if your eye causes you to sin, pluck it out and throw it away; it is better for you to enter life with one eye than to be thrown into the hell of fire" (Matt. 18:8, 9, RSV).

From outward appearances, Sam looked like a nice, but excessively conscientious person. His conscience didn't help him, though. He didn't know God *never* said that the sin of lust is unpardonable. Sam's horror at the thought of committing the unpardonable sin brought him such agony that he feared leaving his room in the morning. He continually told himself what a terrible person he was because of his lust. He told himself he deserved to die, that God certainly hated him. He believed even if God would forgive him his sins, he still would have to die because he would not be free from sin's power. Without changing his misbeliefs, Sam will not be able to accept God's forgiveness or power.

The story has a happy ending. By challenging the lies, Sam learned to tell himself he did not need to cling to his mother for his goals and wants in life to be fulfilled. He then learned it was not too painful to live as an independent person. His fear of responsibility had been so exaggerated that he hid behind

distorted self-talk to keep himself dependent and ir-
responsible.

Understanding What Lust Is

The deadly sin of lust is always and almost exclusively associated with sexual sin. God is not
against sex. He is unequivocally in favor of it. The
idea that sex in itself is sinful is unchristian. The
physical relationship in a marriage is extremely important and holy (Heb. 13:4). Nothing must contam-
inate the physical expression of love between a husband and wife. That is why lust, like a leech, will rob
the sexual relationship of the beauty and joy God
intended in a marriage.

Here is a conversation with one of our counselees:

Jean: I simply cannot stand being married to my
husband anymore. He's not a bad person. In fact, he's
a wonderful person. But I can't tolerate him any
longer.

Therapist: You can't stand him even though he's
a wonderful person?

Jean: He *is* a wonderful person. Everybody says
so. He's kind, honest, sensitive. . . .

Therapist: Is he really all these things if you can't
stand him?

Jean: The thing I cannot stand is that he's just
not *romantic*. I am actually turned off by him. I hate
our sex life. I feel like a mechanical doll and it's driving me crazy.

Therapist: Explain what you mean when you say,
"Driving me crazy."

Jean: I meet other men all the time who turn me
on. I met a man just this week through a girlfriend

at work and we all had lunch together. It was incredible. I could hardly eat while looking at him. My girlfriend left us alone and we immediately gravitated to each other. I knew he felt the same as I. The feeling was lust.

Therapist: Are these the feelings which cause you to think you should leave your husband?

Jean: I just don't want my husband, that's all. Tell me, is it wrong to want to feel like a *woman?* My husband makes me feel I am unattractive. Is it wrong to want to feel good about myself?

This may have been the same kind of self-talk the woman caught in adultery in Jesus' day used (John 8). She was brought before Jesus by a band of scribes and Pharisees as one caught in the flagrant sin of adultery. They hauled her across the temple square, pushing her through the crowd, and hurled her down in front of Jesus. Jesus looked at her with tenderness as she cowered in disgrace and shame before Him. Then He demonstrated His profound wisdom and insight into the human heart.

The scribes and Pharisees had arranged this plot to trick Him; if Jesus confirmed the Mosaic penalty for adultery, He would have had to agree to the woman's execution. Then He could be accused as a relentless censor, striving to revive the penalties of early Judaism. If He refused to confirm the law, He could be put to death as a blasphemer of God's law. The scribes and Pharisees must have been delighted with themselves for devising such a clever plot.

Jesus was just beginning to teach the people when the distraught woman was cast before Him. After hearing the accusations against her, He calmly announced, "He that is without sin among you, let him cast the first stone at her."

Nobody came forward. The men began sheepishly to disperse.

Jesus then turned to the woman and asked, "Hath no man condemned thee?"

The accused woman answered timidly, "No man, Lord."

"Neither do I condemn thee: go, and sin no more."

Jesus always brought love and hope to those who would receive it. He unmasked deception whenever it reared its head. The story of the woman caught in adultery shows us how fearful it is for a sinner to fall into the hands of fellow sinners. F. B. Meyer said sin blinds people to their own faults, but sharpens them to detect the faults of others. If not stoned with stones, a person can be stoned with gossip, ostracization, and all forms of ungodly punishments. If others do not do it, he may punish himself.

The Lord treats sin entirely differently. He is not on the side of ruthless accusers. He loves to respond to a heart that yearns for God's mercy. Accusing voices are hushed in His presence. He condemns the sin and liberates the sinner from his old ways.

The Apostle John writes, "If our heart condemn us, God is greater than our heart" (1 John 3:20). The Lord abolishes self-condemnation of the heart just as He dispersed the mob of scribes and Pharisees who were gloating over the adulteress. Historian Alfred Edersheim wrote, "A Jewish rabbi could not have acted and spoken with such compassion and whole spirit [as Jesus did that day]; he would not have even understood Jesus; nay, a rabbi, however gentle and pitiful, would in word and deed have taken precisely the opposite direction from that of the Christ." St. Gregory observed that this incident in Jewish history is more fit to be wept over than discussed.

In the verse immediately following the above account of the woman caught in adultery, Jesus declares, "I am the light of the world: he that followeth me shall not walk in darkness, but shall have the light of life" (John 8:12). We can walk in God's light, able to resist the temptation to sin as well as the temptation to live in unforgiveness—toward others and ourselves. We use the light of truth. *What we believe is good for us, we will do.*

Paul Wilson, in his book, *The Institution of Marriage,* says, "[Marriage] was a divine plan and a God-given provision for His creatures—man. He who would corrupt this union is guilty of affront to God, and he who despises the relationship despises God who gave it." Lust outside of the marriage or within the marriage corrupts the marriage union.

Jesus taught that lust is not just a physical transgression, it is a defilement of the heart and soul. Satan will always try to plant evil ideas in your mind, no matter how good and moral you are. You will be tempted to lust after someone God has not given to you and you will succumb to the temptation if you are not actively employing the truth in your belief system. Jean, the lady mentioned at the beginning of this chapter, told herself lies until she was thoroughly convinced they were true and good.

When the sin of lust runs free, some of the misbeliefs in residence are, "I am not hurting anybody by what I do," and "I deserve something good and so I'll take what *I* think is good." These are what Potiphar's wife believed as she tried to unleash her lust on Joseph (Gen. 39). He was busy minding his business, managing the house of Potiphar while she was fantasizing about and lusting after him. She finally propositioned Joseph. He recognized immediately the lies of lust and responded, "How then can I do this great wickedness, and sin against God?" Joseph was determined to hold to God's truth. Potiphar's wife eventually had him imprisoned on false charges.

Lust can brew and foment in your mind where you think nobody can see. Eventually it will snare you and you will find yourself taking action on your thoughts. When Satan lulls you into daydreaming about sex, remember how Jesus fought the devil's lies. He countered the lie with the truth: "It is written. . . ." Isaiah wrote, "Thou wilt keep him in perfect peace, whose mind is stayed on thee. . ." (Isa. 26:3). Joseph's choice established his moral character forever. Jesus will give you the power to stay true; He will bless your faithfulness as you refuse the lies of Satan and choose the truth.

Love vs. Lust

The craving which lust implies is often romanticized and called love. Popular music and literature is replete with such "love." Refusal to face our sins, as we have discussed before, leads to neurotic behavior. Many couples are married because of a fear of committing sexual sin outside of marriage. This is not love. The couple becomes physically attracted to one another and develop their appetites and desires for a sexual relationship. When this appetite and desire goes out of control and the desire becomes master, it is called lust, not love.

In Matthew 5, Jesus identifies lust as the basis of distorted sexuality. He says that *looking* at a person lustfully is equivalent to the act of adultery (vv. 27, 28).

But consider some of Jesus' other admonitions.

He says in this same passage of scripture, if we are angry with our brother or call him a fool, we are guilty of murder and deserving of the hell of fire. Both of these scriptures clearly demonstrate we, in our own human strength, are unable to keep ourselves right with God. When Jesus also tells us to love our enemies and pray for those who persecute us, we balk. Jesus tells us to turn our cheek when somebody gives us a slap, to get slapped on the other side; and how do we feel about those words? Jesus tells us to remove an eye or hand if it causes us to sin, and do we actually do that? Happily, the Holy Spirit's power can make us holy.

Looking at a person of the opposite sex does not mean that you have committed sin. You can admire a person and still not be committing sin. If you imagine a physical relationship with that person, you get caught in the snare of fantasizing and can become unable to control your desires. This loss of control can include deviant sexual behavior, and even joking about sex in conversation (treating with lightness something that deserves respect), nurturing an unnatural desire to talk about sex. Engaging in an unbridled appetite for any illicit thing is not funny nor will it be satisfied.

Many people have felt condemned because they looked with lust at another person. It is a miserable, defeating realization that lusting in the heart is actually the same as committing adultery. Why are the two the same? In order to understand this, we must start with these words from Proverbs: "As a man thinketh in his heart, so is he." Lust is sin because it begins in the mind and, if unchecked, is *acted out afterward*. You think because nobody can see your thoughts, you are safe. You think you can fantasize about the woman next door and dream of a sexual relationship with her and that nobody will be the wiser because nobody can see your dreams. But that's not true.

Sexual perverts begin their acts of crime by *thinking* about them. A recent study of pedophiles shows they thought constantly about their heinous acts against small children long before they committed them. Lust begins in daydreams, thoughts, and at-titudes. Jesus said if we have thought about adultery, we have committed it, so we need to stop these thoughts before they stake a claim in our mind. We have God-given power to control the sin of lust. It takes *choice*. We, not our environment, dictate the place of lust in our life. We will not be victims of lust when we can honestly appraise our thoughts and self-talk and bring them directly to the Lord to be Holy Spirit laundered by truth.

God's Design

Physical attraction to one's mate is important. God expects us to love and desire the spouse He gave us. God designed our sex drive to be directed to our spouse *only*. Sex is God's idea and a husband and wife can follow their instincts without fear. For the Christian husband and wife sex is a blending of their love and of their individual personhoods. The Creator intended for us to use sex to express our love for our mate. In his book, *60 Things God Said About Sex,* Lester Sumrall says, "Marriage is the most unique relationship on earth. It is above all other human relationships. Only in marriage do two people share their minds, their souls, and even their bodies. Only in marriage do two people pledge their lifelong loyalty, 'forsaking all others,' as the wedding vow says. Only in marriage do two people join with God to bring other human beings into this world—others who are created in the image of God. Married love is holy because God created the marriage bond."

When you think pleasurable thoughts about your sexual relationship with your spouse, it is not a sin. Don't be deceived into thinking that pleasure is somehow sinful. The carnal world would have us believe that pleasure is the *only* purpose of sex. The Song of Solomon describes the sexual love of a husband and wife for one another. It also symbolizes God's love for His people. Pleasure is part of and a product of the expression of love. It is not just pleasure for pleasure's sake.

"Whether therefore ye eat, or drink, or whatsoever ye do, do all to the glory of God" (1 Cor. 10:31). We were created to enjoy sex *in marriage* and be a tribute to the Lord and His Word. God is glorified by a pure, unrestrained, joyous sex life. The open, unabashed freedom of married sex that flows from *self-giving love* is a joy. It is without guilt. Marital love which is not contaminated or diluted by lust can experience great heights of beauty and blessing.

Lust and the Single Life

If you are a single person, the delights of sex are simply not yours at the present time. There is no way you can study the Word of God with integrity and honesty and find a loophole offering sex outside of marriage. It does not matter if you are divorced or have never married. God is protective of sex.

This does not mean He wants you to be frustrated and unhappy. He knows what is best for you, so He

insists on your following His instruction. He over-
rules any arguments and protests you might raise.
He is fully aware that society preaches free sex is
okay. He knows that most of the people around you
are immoral and that they consider fornication (sex
between unmarried persons) and adultery (extra-
marital sex) normal and acceptable.

Does this put painful restrictions on your life? It
may cause some frustration, but your physical drives
can be controlled by the even stronger force in yourself: your thought life. What are you telling yourself
about sex? Are you telling yourself how miserable it
is to be single and unable to fulfill your sex drive—
if you intend to remain in God's graces? Are you telling yourself that you can't possibly resist a sexual
involvement because sex, after all, is one of man's
basic *needs*? That you can't possibly resist even the
look of lust, which is the same as committing adultery? Are you telling yourself, "It's hopeless. I can't
possibly live up to God's expectations. After all, I'm
only *human*"?

Don't flatter yourself. Don't believe the lie that
your sex drive is uniquely powerful. The truth is,
everyone with normal health is capable of having a
sex life. You are no different than anybody else. You
can control your thoughts about sex as well as you
can control your thoughts about overeating or over-
sleeping. Your sexual appetite is really nothing to
boast about if you're single. Lust can be a problem
for the married as well as the single person.

Often it is good to express your true feelings, but
you do not have to act out all your feelings. It is a lie
that all feelings must be expressed. You can say you
feel that the Joneses' car should be yours, but that
doesn't mean that you must pull out Jones from be-

hind the driver's seat, hurl him into a ditch, and drive off in his car. *You can control your thoughts and self-talk about your so-called needs.*

Single person, be brave and face the fact: you cannot presently have a sex life. You live exclusive of that privilege. You have many freedoms and privileges in your life as a single person but sex is not one of them. You may find yourself a victim of sexual fantasy unless you take time to have a good talk with yourself. Tell yourself, "Self, you are single and you will be in control of your thoughts regarding sex." If you allow yourself to fantasize sexual activities, if you inundate your mind with movies or pictures portraying sex, you will be a victim haunted and most miserable. You will find yourself attracted to people who are also driven by lust; the temptations will be so great that the enticement of lust will displace God's presence in your life.

It is not true that you cannot be fulfilled without sex. If you're a single person, fulfillment without sex is God's standard. God wants you to be completely happy. And happiness has nothing to do with sex. If it did, celibate Jesus would have been an extremely unhappy person.

Marty is thirty-five and single. After fifteen years of marriage, he and his wife were divorced and he found himself living alone and hating it. He felt deprived and emasculated without sex. As he dated several girls in the singles group at his new church, he found most of them had similar frustrations. The women were looking for husbands and felt trapped by God's rules.

"The only way I can have sex is to marry somebody," Marty lamented. "I just got out of one rotten marriage. I'm not ready to jump into another just so

I can have sex. God just isn't fair." Marty was tormented by his desires and felt God had gypped him.

He began to fear his own sexuality, wondering what kind of a man he would become if he lived without having a woman for any period of time. He had been taught from boyhood that a man's sexual prowess is the meter of his total masculinity. As a young man he often had heard his father laughing and joking with friends about sexual feats and conquests. When Marty reached puberty, his father had taken him aside and explained the use of contraceptives so he wouldn't inadvertently get a girl pregnant. When he was thirteen, the other boys his age were already boasting about their sexual exploits. Marty did not know that they were as frightened as he was and that the talk was mostly lies and exaggerations. So he began to exaggerate and lie, also, in order to fit in and be a "man."

Now at thirty-five years old he felt like a eunuch, like a worthless person. He felt the only way he could regain his manhood would be to abandon God; after all, God had hurt him by making fornication a sin.

The Truth About the Single Life

Marty needed to examine his self-talk, most of which was nonsense. A person is not any more a man or woman because of sexual experience. Marty needed to see himself as a *person*, then to allow God to express himself through every area of his life, including his sexuality.

Here are the truths about lust which will set you free:
1. Engaging in sex does not make me a happier, more worthwhile, or less frustrated person.

2. Engaging in sex is not the answer to the needs in my life. Sex is not a need, but a drive, and if God has said sex outside of marriage is forbidden, then He will provide for me the power to live a life of beauty, integrity, strength, and joy—without sex, as long as I am single.
3. I can refuse to bow my knee to anything, including lust, when I have chosen to bow my knee only to the resurrected King of kings, Jesus Christ.
4. I will *not* die if I remain single and celibate. I may not have chosen the single life, but there are many things in this world one would not choose and yet can be happy in spite of. God has promised to supply all my needs, so I consider myself a person with all needs met.
5. If I am unmarried, I am not being deprived. God is generous. He constantly gives and therefore I choose to put myself in a *receiving* frame of mind and take the joy and the rich experiences God has for me as a single person.

Jesus did not come to bleach your life of color, to rob it of delight and joy. He came that your joy might be full. You are complete *in Christ*. Married or single you will find your completeness and fulfillment only in Jesus Christ.

Controlling Your Thought Life

"Bring into captivity every thought to the obedience of Christ" (2 Cor. 10:5). When you catch your mind wandering, before it becomes engulfed by cravings and you become swamped by uncontrolled illicit desires, stop yourself. It is possible for you to control your own thoughts.

You may think you are tormented by some outside force which you have no control over. This is not true. Counteract such self-talk with the truth:

1. "I am not tormented by outside forces over which I have no control. I refuse to dwell on obsessive sexual thoughts, as well as all unhealthy and unclean thoughts."

2. "I can tell myself to stop before I allow a thought to take root in my mind. I can resist the devil and he will flee from me if I am submitting my thoughts to God."

3. "Sex and sex fantasies have no power over me. I have been my own worst enemy and I choose now to be my friend instead. I choose now to think pure and good and holy thoughts."

Thinking good thoughts may take some work if you are not used to it. Start by reading good books, watching wholesome television programs (or turning off the TV permanently), fellowshiping with other Christians who are positive about God and life, praying and studying God's Word regularly.

The Apostle Paul wrote, "For our light affliction, which is but for a moment, worketh for us a far more exceeding and eternal weight of glory" (2 Cor. 4:17). Paul speaks of personal struggles as trivial afflictions. You can renounce sin and self-seeking and have a heightened sense of inner joy, a joy and experience in the Holy Spirit only a single person knows. Paul said, "But I say to the unmarried and to the widows that it is good for them to remain [single] even as I" (1 Cor. 7:8). Paul knew the holiness of God is a blessed gift.

A Testimony of Freedom

A man had been arrested several times for sex crimes. He finally gave his heart to the Lord Jesus and through hard work and much effort on his part, the miraculous and life-giving power of God transformed his life. He does not give his testimony in churches often, because it is not the kind of testimony that wins acceptance. Most would rather hear how someone was healed of a disease than hear how someone was delivered from lust.

He said one day in church with tears streaking down his face, "I cannot explain what it is like to be free from lust. I was driven by such a horrible and hideous monster within me. That monster was *myself*. I was controlled by ugly and unclean thoughts constantly. To be free of these thoughts and this overwhelming drive is more wonderful than I can describe. To wake up with lovely thoughts in the morning is like being in heaven. I no longer have tormenting nightmares. I am free, really free, at last. Jesus has set me free. I'm filled with His Spirit. I'm a totally new person!"

"Therefore if any man be in Christ, he is a new creature: old things are passed away; behold, all things are become new" (2 Cor. 5:17). When a person is born again by the Holy Spirit, he not only is a child of God, he begins to *think* and *act* as a child of God.

CHAPTER TEN

The Problem of Overeating

The sin of gluttony is deadly, because, if pursued, its eventual control over us will affect the power of God in our lives.

In the fifth century Cyril of Alexandria wrote about the gluttons of his day because he was distressed over their behavior. He wrote that it was senseless for people to "besmear their hands with condiments and constantly reach for the sauce." Affluent people of his day shamelessly stuffed themselves with food. The ones St. Cyril found most distasteful were people who "ravenously seized food like swine or dogs." In a burning desire to bloat themselves to the point of agony, they would cram both jaws at once. As they ate, perspiration slid down their faces onto their clothes and into their plates. Their

129

insatiable greed, as St. Cyril understated, showed them to be "preoccupied with food."

The Finicky Eater

You may think gluttony doesn't pertain to you because you are very finicky about what you eat. You hardly eat a thing. Maybe you excuse yourself with, "I hate to eat." This is gluttony, because the deadly sin of gluttony is *preoccupation with food*, period. A glutton focuses day and night attention on food, whether he or she eats it or not.

Many people of average weight have sought counsel in order to overcome gluttonous habits. "I think about food constantly," said Delores, an attractive woman in her twenties. "I'm finicky about food. I eat only health foods, but I feel as if I'm pigging out at every meal. Then I starve myself. Food is an obsession with me. I despise junk food, so I've been a vegetarian for two years. But I eat constantly. I have to run at least five miles a day to burn up the excess calories I consume."

Beautiful Delores is a glutton.

Mel, a slender 35-year-old businessman, eats only the finest foods. When he travels, he special orders his meals on airplanes. He refuses traditional dishes and dines exclusively on exotic foods prepared by either himself in his gourmet kitchen or by the best chefs in the restaurants he favors. His life centers around food. He spends countless hours shopping for and preparing food. A dinner party at Mel's is an experience people don't forget.

Mel, though slim, is a glutton.

Other Types of Gluttony

We can include under the category of gluttony such things as alcohol and drug abuse, and cigarette smoking—anything to which a person bows the knee because he thinks he *must* have it. If a person desires to consume something with little thought for anything or anyone else, he is gluttonous. The object of the gluttony becomes an idol, and God is pushed far off into the background.

If you are a glutton you believe what you crave is *good* for you. When you are tempted to drink too much, your self-talk is, "Oh, this won't hurt me. It'll be fun!" When you desperately cling to a relationship as though your life depended upon the other person's presence and approval, your self-talk is, "Having him/her as my own and being totally in control of him/her would be *good* for me." When you break your diet and go on an eating binge, your self-talk is, "This food tastes so good; it'll be *good* for me to have it. I can't deny myself something so good."

A major lie of gluttony is, "I must have what I want because it will make me happy, even if it's bad for me." The devil cannot possibly trip a person until he is persuaded something is true which is actually false. Many times in a *Free To Be Thin** group, we will hear words such as, "I have a weak will and I just can't help myself where food is concerned." This of course is not true. God has given each person a will with which to carry out his own choices.

---

*Free To be Thin by Marie Chapian with Neva Coyle (Bethany House Publishers) describes the weight-loss program used by Overeaters Victorious.

The Benefits of a Weak Will

Rosemary tells herself she is too weak to change. She finds safety in her conviction that she is weak-willed. When you act like a weak person, people will not expect you to do such things as stay on a weight-loss program, or a fitness regimen. If others are convinced you are not responsible for your own behavior, they will never expect you to do what you say you will do, or to control yourself in any manner. You don't have to change, because nobody expects you to. You have convinced people that God is at fault for not giving you a stronger will.

Rosemary indulged in gluttony much like a newborn baby who wants what he wants when he wants it, and if he doesn't get it he will scream until he does. The difference between the newborn baby and Rosemary's behavior is that the newborn baby is behaving exactly as he is supposed to.

If gluttony has been your problem, tell yourself you are finished with the old childish ways and ready to begin some mature Christian habits. You're ready to believe the truth. Rosemary learned to believe the truth: *"It is not good to be weak. It is not good for me to have exactly what I want when I want it."*

Eating and the Sense of Worthlessness

Lisa, twenty-eight years old, frequently cries when she talks about her life because she is so ashamed of herself. As she dabs her eyes, she says, "I don't know what I'm going to do. I keep telling myself I'll get up at 6:30 and fix breakfast for my husband, but when 6:30 comes I pretend I don't hear the alarm and go right back to sleep. When I finally get out of bed I prepare my coffee just in time for the daily soap operas. I tell myself I'll watch just one and then get to my housework, but I watch them all. When I realize that the day is more than half gone, I'm so disgusted with myself that I prepare myself something to eat in order to feel better. I don't stop with bacon and eggs or one sandwich; I eat six sandwiches or six eggs and a half loaf of bread. I don't see any way out of this thing. I feel totally helpless and worthless."

Ed is a top salesman in a national company, but for the last six months he hasn't called on any clients and hasn't pursued new prospects. He phones old accounts but is not bringing in any new business. He tells himself that calling on prospective customers has begun to cause him too much stress. Every time he makes a visit, he gets an uncomfortable feeling in his stomach. When that happens he finds it nearly impossible to force himself to proceed with the appointment.

Ed explains in despair, "I can't sleep because I'm depressed and worried, so I get up early—much too early to visit anyone in his office. I therefore treat myself to the biggest breakfast I can find. Then as I prepare to make the calls I'm supposed to, I tell myself, 'I don't think this is the day for calling on people. Maybe they're not in on Monday anyhow. I'll try tomorrow.' Soon it's lunchtime and I decide I can't do anything while everybody's having his lunch, so I go to another restaurant and eat. I've eaten as many as three lunches in three different restaurants."

Evelyn does not go shopping because she feels insecure about shopping alone. When she wants to go to the store, she calls Stan, her husband, asking him to come home from work because she feels tense and anxious. She convinces him he must come home to help her. He must answer her every need. She tells him tearfully, "I can't stand being in the stores all alone. Don't you realize how I *need* you?"

Do you observe a similarity in the lives of these three people? The gluttonous lie they each believe is, "I *must* have what I want." Pleasure and comfort sit at the top of their needs list.

If you are telling yourself, "I don't have any self-control; I'm a spineless jellyfish," you must realize and admit the lie before you can be free. If gluttony is your problem, if you believe that you can't give up something, that you can't quit smoking, that you can't give up drunkenness or a demanding or illicit relationship, that you can't stop overeating, there are some useful steps you should take to disprove that notion:

1. *Acknowledge your condition.* Once you have acknowledged that your behaviors are gluttonous, you can begin to be free. The Holy Spirit will lead you into all truth. He will empower you by providing the truth for the situation. You then must use the truth God has shown.

2. *Realize how important you are to God* and how much He wants you to overcome sin. If you practice sin, which destroys, you apparently consider yourself of no value.

3. *Look beyond momentary gratification.* Find yourself a comfortable chair, sit down and imagine yourself saying no to the temptation you're having trouble with. Live through the moment of temptation. Tell yourself, "I don't need this momentary thrill. It is a lie that it would be good for me."

4. *Learn to identify Satan's voice.* Satan, the en-

emy of God, tries to convince you to engage in some behavior that will ultimately hurt you. He *never* tells the whole truth. He can't. He is a liar. You will always feel compelled to comfort yourself with something that will harm you if you are acting on a lie of Satan.

5. *Learn to identify God's voice.* God will always tell you the truth.

Why do we resist God's Word and the power of God within us? There are at least two reasons:

1. We refuse to help ourselves change because we believe that what we want is far more important than anything else in the world—even more important than what God wants, even though only He knows what is best for us.

2. We believe it will be too difficult to change. Certainly living without any rules or discipline is easy, but it lacks joy. "Blessed [happy] is the man that walketh not in the counsel of the ungodly" (Ps. 1:1). Let the sinner live as a sinner; we must live as persons empowered with the Holy Spirit and stand against the things intended to destroy us.

We are free to be fulfilled by God. Gluttony forfeits that freedom, leaving us bound to continue sinning—"One more chocolate eclair will make me happy." But we are temples of the Holy Spirit, dwellings of God, and dead to sin.

CHAPTER ELEVEN

Dead to Sin

God loves a happy heart. We teach ourselves to be happy by knowing who we are in the eyes of God. According to St. Thomas Aquinas, the essence of truth is to attain to the love of God, and know His benefits; then the more we know His benefits, the more we shall love Him. A right relationship with God comes from realizing and acting on the benefits and privileges He gives us. Apart from God there are no benefits. The humanistic writer Thoreau said, "Men wander through their lives in quiet desperation." Is that any way to live?

We have discussed in this book how to identify our self-talk, to question it and to replace it if it is based on misbeliefs. With such knowledge, and God's grace, we are able to change. Without change we are like mules carrying cargoes of precious jewels and perfume. Although we are carrying these precious items, they have no effect on us whatsoever.

The seven deadly sins are the results of refusal to change. It is pride that refuses God's love and mercy. It is envy that hates seeing anyone else receive blessing. It is anger that fights back at every hint or semblance of personal affront. It is lust that corrupts the beauty of marriage which is the symbol of Christ's love for His Church. It is greed that keeps us bound to continual dissatisfaction. It is sloth that numbs the mind and will with sorrow. It is gluttony that seeks to be comforted without God. You can consider yourself humble by being quiet and reserved, but true humility is to accept and receive all that God gives you.

Freedom from the seven deadly sins requires learning lifetime skills and strategies of warfare, of victorious self-talk. The following are examples of self-talk that result in victory over sin:

"I give people the right to reject or accept me."

"I give others the right to be better at what they do than I."

"I give people the right to dress better than I do."

"I do not need all the things I think I need."

"I can trust God to know what is best for me."

"I do not need what others have."

"I am as important to God as someone else."

"I forgive those who have wronged me."

"I forgive myself."

"I am going to be happy today."

"I *can* help the way I feel and choose to be in control of my feelings."

The Word of God says we are to work righteousness and speak the truth in our hearts (Ps. 15:2). We can overcome sin and display the character of Christ as living proof that "the truth shall make you free."

God's Pardon

God is a forgiver. "And by him all that believe are justified from all things, from which ye could not be justified by the law of Moses" (Acts 13:39). We are justified from all things, not because we are so good, but because we belong to Jesus if we have repented and received Him. God makes no exceptions in His offer of salvation.

Then what is the unpardonable sin? We have looked at the seven deadly sins. Are any of them unpardonable? The Bible says no.

One of the most amazing records of God's forgiveness is found in 1 Cor. 6:9-11. In it the Apostle Paul lists the kinds of people who will not enter His kingdom: fornicators, idolators, adulterers, effeminate, homosexuals, thieves, coveteous, drunkards, revilers and extortioners. He then says to the believers, "*And such were some of you:* But ye are washed, but ye are sanctified, but ye are justified in the name of the Lord Jesus, and by the Spirit of our God." None of these sins were unpardonable.

When we repent and ask for forgiveness, we will not be refused. "If we confess our sins, he is faithful and just to forgive us our sins. . ." (1 John 1:9). There's only one solution for sin-guilt and that is forgiveness and cleansing. God is a forgiving God. He pardons our sins.

Murder is not unpardonable. David confessed his sin and was forgiven (Ps. 32:5).

Theft is not unpardonable. The penitent thief on the cross was pardoned (Luke 23:43).

Blasphemy is not unpardonable. Paul was a blasphemer and he was pardoned (1 Tim. 1:13).

Adultery is not unpardonable. The woman of Samaria was saved (John 4:7–42).

Unrepentance is the only unpardonable sin.

To repent of our sins does not mean that we torture ourself in agony over them. God will not forgive any better if we make ourselves miserable. He does not judge our emotions. It is good to weep over our sins, but God hears and loves our prayers whether tearful or not.

Once we have repented we are free. "I am crucified with Christ: nevertheless I live; yet not I, but Christ liveth in me: and the life which I now live in the flesh I live by the faith of the Son of God, who loved me, and gave himself for me" (Gal. 2:20). We no longer have to follow the dictates of our emotions or hormones, for Jesus is living His triumphant life in us. We are now dead to sin. We can "reckon . . . [our]selves to be dead indeed unto sin, but alive unto God through Jesus Christ our Lord" (Rom. 6:11). In this case "reckon" means to consider or calculate. In other words, even if we don't feel dead to sin, we are.

The devil and our human nature sometimes influence us with thoughts such as, "You can't ever change. This is too big for you. You've tried before, what makes you think you'll win this time?" To counter this onslaught, we resist the devil with truth and he will flee from us (James 4:7). We are led by the Spirit (Gal. 5:18). We are more than conquerors through Christ Jesus (Rom. 8:37), and furthermore we are dead to sin. *We can overcome sin. There is no sin you cannot overcome, because you have the power of the Holy Spirit within you. It is up to you to take this power and overcome! The freedom and victory are yours.*

Books by Marie Chapian

POETRY:
City Psalms (Moody Press, 1972)
Mind Things (Creation House, 1973)

GIFT BOOKS:
To My Friend Books (Successful Living, 1974)

CHILDREN'S BOOKS:
Mustard Seed Library (Creation House, 1974)
    The Holy Spirit and Me
    I Learn About the Fruit of the Holy Spirit
    I Learn About the Gifts of the Holy Spirit

BIOGRAPHY:
Help Me Remember/Help Me Forget (Bethany House, 1975, Previously titled, *The Emancipation of Robert Sadler*)
Of Whom the World Was Not Worthy (Bethany House, 1978)
In the Morning of My Life (Tyndale House, 1979)
Escape From Rage (Bridge, 1981)

CHRISTIAN LIVING:
Free To Be Thin with Neva Coyle (Bethany House, 1979)
Telling Yourself the Truth with Dr. William Backus (Bethany House, 1980)
Fun To Be Fit (Fleming Revell, 1983)
Love and Be Loved (Fleming Revell, 1983)
There's More To Being Thin Than Being Thin with Neva Coyle (Bethany House, 1984)
Staying Happy in an Unhappy World (Fleming Revell, 1984)
Why Do I Do What I Don't Want to Do? with Dr. William Backus (Bethany House, 1984)